FINNISH EDUCATION IN PRACTICE

•

What, Why and How

Design & Layout by Kite Group
www.kitegroup.com.mt
info@kitegroup.com.mt

First published in 2021 by Kite Group, Malta
in collaboration with Learning Scoop, Finland

Printed by Print It, Malta

ISBN 978-9918-23014-3

FINNISH EDUCATION IN PRACTICE

•

What, Why and How

Johanna Järvinen-Taubert, Päivi Valtonen &
Elena Chukhlantseva
Editors

Kite

Kite Group
Outstanding, innovative and cutting-edge are the hallmarks of Kite Group, Malta. Kite has a thirst for new material. At Kite Group we commit ourselves to exclusive, well-researched and well-written content, professional and creative design, excellent presentation, and high-quality printing. As a publishing house we strive to create an enjoyable and enriching experience to authors and readers.

Learning Scoop
Learning Scoop is a Finnish company working in the fields of teacher education and pedagogical leadership. Learning Scoop experts consists of experienced Finnish teachers, teacher trainers and educators who have empowered teachers and principals around the world.

CONTENTS

FOREWORD

As an ambassador and a school principal with a history of collaborating with several Finnish entities for a number of years and facilitating the visits of international educators in Finland, it is a pleasure and an honor to be given the opportunity to write this foreword. The title of this book, *Finnish Education in Practice: What Why and How*, definitely confirms that a publication such as this should be an essential reference resource for all policy makers, teachers and senior leaders alike. The publication helps its readers learn more about the Finnish education system as it effectively provides them with detailed insight about the country and its educational progression during the past decade.

In fact, educators interested in international research are certainly aware of the extensive progress Finland has gained in various educational areas over the past few years. This country has not only been recognized as offering quality education at higher levels with optimum results but has also obtained excellent results in international examinations such as PISA, PIRLS and TIMSS. Consequently, educators and policymakers across the world have taken a special interest in the Finnish education system and its characteristics.

There are certain characteristics which make the Finnish educational system original and unique, all of which are mentioned and discussed in this very publication. The recently introduced curriculum for Finnish schools is also now reflected in the teaching and assessment of students of different ages; in the type of counseling and welfare services offered to students; in the opportunity to teach outside of the classroom; and in the structure and administration of various Finnish educational institutions. Considering this aspect, I would also like to refer to the two basic principles which are constantly emphasized by Finnish educational policymakers and educators: the promotion of collaboration instead of competition and the need for students to learn principles which they will eventually utilize in their life and in the outside world.

In order to reach such principles, the lessons and activities in Finland focus on the learner. Group work, collaboration and cooperation are expected not only from the students but also from the educators. Neither the students nor the educators are expected to work in isolation. Heads of School are expected to implement a number of leadership styles, especially that of a pedagogical style of leadership. In contrast to some other Western and Asian countries, Finland does not believe in teaching in order to perform well in a test. Instead, children are taught the skills that they would need to succeed in life and to be productive, independent and autonomous learners. Educators are expected to instruct or to guide those who experience difficulties with a task. This is because teachers, who are considered to be trusted professionals, constantly prioritize the concept of how to learn instead of what to learn.

In a similar manner, Finland recently introduced the concept of phenomenon-based learning. As a former Minister of Education put it during a discussion we had some years ago, one of the reasons why this introduction was possible is that the country has highly educated, skilled and motivated teachers. The teaching profession is respected, and teachers of all school levels are highly qualified and committed. Universities can select among the most motivated and talented applicants. Highly qualified teachers who constantly update and improve their competence are also trusted with a great deal of independence and autonomy. Finnish teachers have considerable freedom in choosing their teaching methods and textbooks. This also enables learner-centeredness.

The open atmosphere that exists in Finnish schools supports creativity and innovation. Attention is paid to the diverse personal development of children, while educators and senior leaders work to ensure a balance between theoretical, vocational and scientific subjects as well as arts and crafts. This also shows that a holistic perspective on children's well-being is considered to be critical in this country. School days are not only for academic skills but also for physical education, developing one's social skills and learning to live and act as members of a community.

These are all aspects and themes which are highly discussed and analyzed in the different chapters and sections of this publication. I strongly believe that *Finnish Education in Practice: What, Why and How* compliments other publications on Finnish educational theory and pedagogy researched and published during the past decade. Finally, I would like to thank and congratulate Johanna Järvinen-Taubert, Päivi Valtonen and Elena Chukhlantseva, the editors of this book who, together with other Finnish educational specialists and teachers, share their expertise and good practices through such an inspiring and well-researched publication.

Dr Kenneth Vella
Ambassador of the Republic of Malta to Estonia and Finland

9 April 2021

PREFACE

For several years, there has been great interest towards Finnish education. Teachers, principals and other education experts from many countries have been intrigued about Finland's excellent learning results in international learning comparisons, such as PISA. Not only has Finland managed to combine top learning results with a stress-free and child-centered approach, but Finland has also provided this quality education to all children equally.

The success of the Finnish education system has raised interest around the world. Many teachers, principals and education planners would like to know how this world-famous education system is implemented *in practice*. What do the Finns actually do to achieve such excellent learning results?

With our company, Learning Scoop, we have been training international educators from over 50 different countries by introducing various aspects of Finnish education. Through this work, we have gained insight about which factors of Finnish education are of greatest interest to education experts on a global scale. Since we in Finland have ideas and practices that interest education professionals in other countries, it is natural to share our experiences. For us, sharing is caring.

Several great books about Finnish education have been published during the last few years. What was still missing, though, was a practice-oriented publication of Finnish education that would combine the overall description of certain key topics (*what*), the rationale behind the typical features of Finnish education (*why*) along with practical examples of how these undertakings are implemented in everyday schoolwork (*how*). With this book, we hope to address this need. This book is not, however, a catalog of educational practices to be copied as such in other countries. Education is always tightly intertwined with local context, culture and history. Nevertheless, it is possible to acquire new ideas from other countries and try and apply them to fit one's own country and system. Finland has learned an abundance from other countries while creating the education system we have today. For us, learning from each other is the way to develop education globally.

The book comprises six main articles that present the key topics of Finnish education:

1. The Cornerstones of Finnish Education
2. The New Finnish National Core Curriculum: From Why to How
3. Educational Support in the Finnish Way
4. Finnish Pedagogical Leadership
5. Finnish Early Childhood Education as a Foundation for the Life-Long Learning Path
6. What Should Parents Know About Their Child's Learning – a Finnish Perspective

Each of these main articles includes several practice-oriented case examples that describe multiple practical applications of the leading ideas and objectives in Finnish education. The case examples are written by experienced Finnish education experts: class teachers, subject teachers, special education teachers, principals, teacher trainers and educators.

Each professional who contributed to this project has years of work experience and practical knowledge of the themes they address in this book. This fact makes the book particularly relevant to the audience looking for authentic first-hand information about how the discussed matters work in a real-life education context. All authors have carefully selected their topics, which provide the reader with the most up-to-date developments in Finnish education. For understandable reasons, it is hardly feasible to address the entire range of possible topics (even if we would have loved to 😊).

We want to thank team Learning Scoop for their irreplaceable help with writing this book: thank you Satu Herrala, Riitta Juusenaho, Johanna Kämäräinen, Juha Lahtinen, Jukka Miettunen, Teemu Nieminen, Tommi Roininen and Kaisa Tuomarla for your expertise, passion and flexibility! Thank you for being the best possible team! Huge thanks go to Dr Kenneth

Vella: this book would not have been possible without your constant support. Big thanks also to Iiris Lilja for the professional and flexible help with the translation and editing work. We also owe thanks to our CEO Ellimaija Ahonen for the endless encouragement and perseverance which helped us finalize this script! We also thank Kitc Group for their trust and help in the process.

In addition, we want to thank all the teachers, principals and education experts we have trained both in Finland and abroad. You are an inspiration to us as we strive for our common goal: quality education for all!

Johanna Järvinen-Taubert
Päivi Valtonen
Elena Chukhlantseva

4 April 2021
In Tampere

1

THE CORNERSTONES OF FINNISH EDUCATION

Johanna Järvinen-Taubert (M.Ed.), Pedagogical Director, Learning Scoop, Tampere, Finland

Finnish education is famous for its high quality. Finnish students have been at the top of international rankings for over fifteen years. Experts from all over the world have wondered what makes Finnish education so successful. What could the world learn from Finland?

Understanding Finnish education requires comprehending a few basic principles. These principles lay the basis for the whole education system and education practices in Finland, which this introductory article of this publication presents. Understanding the principles presented here – or the cornerstones, as we call them – is a prerequisite for understanding the organisation and practices of Finnish education. Pasi Sahlberg (2007, 163) states the same idea: *"International student achievement comparison studies are often absorbed by politicians simply by looking at the rank tables of countries, rather than by trying to learn about national underlying characteristics that might explain comparative system performance."*

Finnish education is based on these cornerstones:
1. Equality and equity
2. Trust and responsibility
3. Autonomy
4. Co-operation
5. Learner-centeredness
6. Research-based.

Equality and equity

Equal society

Without question, one of the key words in Finnish education is equality. The emphasis on equality is very much at the center of all the Nordic welfare societies. Finnish society as a whole is based on the idea that every individual should have equal possibilities and be entitled to support according to their needs. One might even say that Finland is not only pursuing equality (giving everyone the same things) but also equity (giving individuals what they need; fairness in every situation). This idea of equal chances and fairness is widely approved in Finland by almost everyone. Of course, the interpretation of how this equality should be carried out may differ.

The Nordic countries are not famous for income inequality but rather for providing decent living for all citizens. Taxation in all the Nordic countries, including Finland, is relatively high. It is also progressive, so those who earn more also pay more in taxes. In return, Finns get free education and nearly free healthcare in addition to many other services from the government. In Finland, this striving towards a decent living conditions for all citizens is also seen as a guarantee for a flourishing society. Hargreaves and Shirley (2008, 137) point out that a strong welfare state is a central part of the Finnish narrative that supports and sustains a successful economy as well.

The Nordic countries are also known for gender equality. As an example, Finnish women were the first in the world[1] to fully exercise the right to vote and the right to stand as candidates in elections in 1907. Even today, Finland has one of the highest percentages of women in national parliament when compared to the whole world. Furthermore, in Finland it is almost taken for granted that the government should have an equal amount of female and male ministers.

Education is strongly intertwined with society's values and culture. Sahlberg (2006, 278) states that education systems operate as an interconnected part of wider social and political systems. The idea of everybody being equal can also be seen in the Finnish education system. One of the fundamental cornerstones of Finnish education is that all people must have equal access to high-quality education and training. The same educational opportunities

[1] Women in New Zealand and Australia won the right to vote before their Finnish counterparts. However, Finnish women were the first in Europe to win the right to vote and the first in the world to have their eligibility for office recognized, i.e. to be able stand as candidates at elections.

should be available to all citizens irrespective of their ethnic origin, age, wealth or their place of residence. (Finnish Education in a Nutshell 2017, 6.) In this perspective, it is little wonder that the typical public debate over any education reform in Finland is focused on the question: Does it promote equality?

• • •

One of the fundamental cornerstones of Finnish education is that all people must have equal access to high-quality education and training.

• • •

Social equality

For Finns, ensuring that all children have equal chances to succeed in education despite their social and financial background is a crucial goal. Sahlberg (2017, XIV–XV) points out that this principle can be seen in Finnish classrooms as well: *"The majority of Finnish pupils study in socially mixed classes without being tracked or segregated by their ability or socio-economic status."*

One main tool for guaranteeing this social equality is the publicly organised[2] education that is free at all levels, all the way from pre-primary to higher education. In pre-primary and basic education, textbooks or other study materials, daily meal and transportation for students who live further away from the school are free for the parents. At upper secondary level and in higher education, either the students themselves or their parents purchase the books, but there are no tuition fees and the education otherwise is free of charge. Additionally, Finland has a well-developed system of study grants and loans to ensure the opportunity to study for everyone. The Finnish government can award financial aid for full-time studies at an upper secondary school, vocational institution or institution of higher education. (Finnish Education in a Nutshell 2017, 6.)

[2] There are few private schools in Finland (mainly based on religion or some alternative pedagogy), but they also follow the national core curriculum, are funded by the government and are not allowed to have tuition fees (Finnish Education in a Nutshell 2017, 10–11).

Gender equality

In Finland, it is self-evident that both boys and girls have the equal rights to education and that they are taught together in same schools. In fact, girls have outperformed boys in education in Finland. The OECD's PISA (Program for International Student Assessment) test results in 2016 showed that Finland is the only country where there are significantly more girls than boys among top performers in science (OECD 2016, 80). According to the 2015 Trends in International Mathematics and Science Study (TIMSS), Finnish fourth-grade girls outperform boys in both mathematics and science (Mullis & al. 2015). Nevertheless, Finns see this as a gender equality issue as well; currently there is an on-going national conversation in Finland about whether the schools are supporting boys enough.

Students with special needs

The equality principle is not limited to pupils and students with different social and financial backgrounds, or to gender issues. In fact, equality is very much the reason why Finland has invested so much in supporting pupils and students with different learning difficulties. Every pupil and student in Finland has the right to educational support.

The current thinking in Finland is that the potential of each pupil should be maximized. This requires educational guidance and counseling. The aim of guidance and counseling is to support, help and guide pupils and students so that they can all perform as well as possible in their studies and be able to make appropriate decisions concerning their education and careers. (Finnish Education in a Nutshell 2017, 7–8.)

All teachers, as well as other education personnel, are responsible for guidance and counseling in Finland. Teachers are required to treat pupils and students as individuals and help them proceed according to their own capabilities. Furthermore, all pupils and students have the right to educational support. This support can be remedial instruction or support for the pupil's special needs. The goal is that every learner could experience success and the joy of learning. (Finnish Education in a Nutshell 2017, 7–8.)

Language minorities and migrants

Even though Finland's population is usually known to be fairly homogenous, Finland also has to take language or ethnic minorities and migrants into account when equality is considered. In Finland, extensive efforts have been made to support language minorities and migrants. Finland has two official languages, Finnish and Swedish, and education is provided in both languages. Approximately five percent of students in basic and upper secondary education attend a school where Swedish is the language of instruction. Higher education is also available in both languages, Finnish and Swedish. (Finnish Education in a Nutshell 2017, 8.)

The right to study one's own mother tongue is taken into account with smaller language groups as well. Local authorities are required to organize education in the Sami language in Sami-speaking areas of Lapland. Education providers can apply for additional funding from the government for organizing instruction in languages such as Romani and Sami, and also for organizing instruction in the migrant pupils' mother tongue. Preparatory education for all migrants is organized to enable them to enter basic or upper secondary education. (Finnish Education in a Nutshell 2017, 8–9.)

It is worth noting that equality is not only a narrative about Finnish education. Equality also takes many practical forms in Finnish education: it turns into various political decisions as well as practical solutions in the everyday life of Finnish schools.

Trust and responsibility

The feature that usually strikes foreign visitors the most in the Finnish educational system is trust (see Hargreaves 2009, 94; Hargreaves & Shirley 2008, 137). Trust is intertwined throughout the Finnish education system and can be found at its every level. Parents trust the teachers and the whole school system. Politicians and authorities trust education providers, education providers trust principals and teachers, principals trust their teachers, teachers trust their students and students trust their teachers and so on.

It is noteworthy that private schools do not practically exist in Finland; most schools are public. This has a special effect on the teacher-parent relationship. Since parents do not pay tuition fees, they are not considered as clients but partners. In Finland, there is a concept of "educational partnership" *(kasvatuskumppanuus)* to describe that the school and parents are on the same side aiming to foster the child's growth together. This idea of shared goals and partnership sustains the very existence of trust. Common aims are best pursued with mutual trust and respect.

Of course, the situation is not exclusively rosy. Currently, there are parents who have various expectations and even demands for the school and its teachers, but the general atmosphere remains that by trusting each other and co-operating, the school and parents are most likely to achieve their common objectives, which is the best for the children. Walker (2017, 122–123) states that Finland's administrators and parents trust the nation's teachers because they respect their professionalism.

This trust is very visible in the administration of education as well. Finland's National Board of Education sets the National Core Curriculum, which determines the outlines of education in Finland alongside other legislation. However, the execution of the curriculum is the task of the local administration and educational institutes, and the National Board of Education trusts that the local parties will play their role well. The activities of education providers are guided by objectives set out in legislation. (Finnish Education in a Nutshell 2017, 12–13.)

There is no school inspection in Finland[3]; instead, quality assurance is based on steering, collaboration and process evaluation instead of controlling. Steering is done through information, support and funding. The system relies on the proficiency and conscientiousness of teachers and other personnel. (Finnish Education in a Nutshell 2017, 12–13.) Pokka (2015, 82–83) points out, that this steering and mutual collaboration has created an atmosphere of trust between education authorities and schools. Authorities trust that by giving resources and guidance to schools and teachers, they will find a way to solve the problems (Walker 2017, 179).

A lack of standardized national testing systems is also a sign of trust in Finland. There are no standardized national tests in Finnish basic education. The evaluation criteria are described in the Finnish National Core Curriculum. The schools and teachers are trusted to justly and truthfully evaluate the learning outcomes of their students based on the criteria. However, there is one form of national evaluation of students in Finland. These regularly executed evaluations are sample-based, and the education providers receive their own results which are then used for development purposes. The main purpose of the national evaluations of learning outcomes is to follow how well the curriculum objectives have been reached at national level and how we should develop education nationally. Therefore, the results are never used for ranking the schools, teachers or students. (Finnish Education in a Nutshell 2017, 13–14.)

[3] The inspections of schools as well as textbooks and other learning materials were abolished in 1990s in Finland (Pokka 2015, 82–83).

Sahlberg (2007, 157) describes the many positive impacts that this culture of trust of letting teachers and principals participate in school development has had on the Finnish education sector:

> *Teachers could see that the system believed that schools and communities are the places where decisions concerning the curriculum and overall arrangement of schooling should be made. Teachers, with their high professional and moral qualifications, mostly welcomed this new responsibility. Also, schools very quickly embraced their new roles in leading change within the culture of trust. School improvement not only emerged in Finland as a consequence of this new trust, but also became much more diverse than earlier. Each school, at least in theory, could design its own change strategy with mission statements, vision and implementation methodologies, and schedules. This dimension of trust has played the most significant role in propelling Finland's education system past those of many other nations.* (Sahlberg 2007, 157.)

This lack of school inspection and teacher assessment in Finland often raises questions among foreign visitors: how are the schools and teachers held accountable, then? It is interesting that Finns practically never use the word "accountability" when they refer to education. In Finland, teachers and schools are *responsible* for their work, not *held accountable* for their actions. Timothy Walker (2017, 121) summarizes this attitude well:

> *Through teaching in Helsinki and interviewing Finnish teachers, I kept hearing the word "responsibility" repeated. I wasn't used to hearing this word in conversations with American educators. Instead, the substitute word I heard most often in the United States was accountability. Although educators in Finland aren't held accountable by standardized tests or school inspections, I'd argue that this low level of accountability works in Finnish schools because there's a high level of professional responsibility, which is afforded by a high level of professional trust.* (Walker 2017, 121.)

●●●

In Finland, teachers and schools are responsible for their work, not held accountable for their actions.

●●●

Walker (2017, 122) makes a good distinction between the two terms: "accountability" is basically fear-based whereas "responsibility" is trust-based. Responsibility empowers those who do the actual work: it offers teachers a strong sense of professional initiative (cf. Sahlberg 2007, 155).

Being responsible for your work is an *inner* demand, posed by the education community and the person themselves. It means knowing that your work has consequences and other parties have expectations for it. Responsibility is an inner calling to do your work as well as possible. Accountability on the other hand is always placed on you by someone else. This operator who holds you accountable for your actions is superior to you and therefore has the final responsibility for your work as well.

Autonomy

One sign of trust is the high level of pedagogical autonomy that teachers have in Finland. Finnish teachers are highly educated and thus considered as experts in their own work. As in any other expert profession, teachers are trusted to know how to conduct their work. They are not inspected or monitored in any manner. Teachers are considered to know best what is good for their pupils and students.

Viewing teaching as a high-expertise profession is the basis for professional autonomy. Experts are not told and supervised; they are expected to carry responsibility over their own work and developing it. In Finland, teachers are professionals in their schools and therefore actively involved in planning and implementing changes in their work. Because Finnish teachers are not externally reviewed, they are free to focus on developing understanding, fostering interest in learning and cultivating open, trust-based relationships between teachers and students. (Sahlberg 2006, 281–282.)

This high-level professionalism of teachers is based on their high-quality education. Teachers are well-educated in Finland: they all graduate from research-based university programs and have a Master's degree. Finnish teacher education is not restricted to the taught subjects and subject didactics only. In addition, newly-graduated teachers have studied child psychology, pedagogy, special education, the current curriculum and societal issues concerning education. These broad educational competencies prepare them for broader professional responsibilities in their schools. Teachers are expected to collectively design their school curricula, choose the most effective ways to teach, assess their students' learning, plan the needed support for students that are struggling, and self-direct their own professional development and growth as teachers. (Sahlberg 2017b, XV.)

Treating teachers as experts and granting them freedom and responsibility over their own work has strengthened the public image of the teaching profession (see Sahlberg 2015, 105). Young people see teaching as an expert profession, and therefore teaching is a very wanted future career in Finland. Top students want to become teachers, which is why it is extremely difficult to be admitted to teacher education. In fact, only 10–20% of the applicants get in. Sahlberg (2017, XV) concludes that the continuous strengthening of the teaching profession in Finland has built a strong and notable trust in teachers and schools, which in turn has further enhanced the status of teachers and the attractiveness of becoming a teacher among young Finns.

The professionalism and autonomy of teachers are tightly intertwined. Sahlberg (2015, 105) states that Finnish teachers at all levels of schooling expect to be given the full professional autonomy that they need to practice what they have been educated to do: to plan, teach, diagnose, take action and evaluate. To be able to follow their commitment professionally, the experts must have access to the resources their work requires. Finnish teachers expect that they are provided with enough time to accomplish all the goals in their work, both inside and outside the normal classroom duties (Sahlberg 2015, 105).

Teachers are truly free in their own classes. Sahlberg (2007, 152) points out that a typical feature of teaching and learning in Finland is encouraging teachers and students to try new ideas and methods, learn about and through innovations, and cultivate creativity in schools while respecting schools' pedagogic legacies.

Teachers have a broad pedagogical autonomy. Based on the curriculum, teachers can decide on matters such as:

1. what they want to emphasize in their teaching,
2. when they teach certain topics,
3. how they teach them,
4. where they teach them,
5. what methods they use in teaching,
6. which subjects and topics they decide to integrate,
7. how they organize the work during lessons,
8. what teaching materials (textbooks, digital materials etc.) they use,

9. how much and what kind of homework[4] they assign to their students,
10. how they evaluate and assess learning, and
11. how they want to collaborate with other teachers.
(See also Finnish Education in a Nutshell 2017, 12–13; Walker 2017, 43–44.)

Walker (2017, 91–127) describes autonomy as one of the key elements in Finnish education. But it is not just the teachers who have autonomy: Finnish pupils and students are very autonomous as well. The young people in Finland are more independent than their peers in many other countries. They are also given more responsibility over their studies. Walker (2017, 93) writes that Finnish children have many opportunities at home and at school to do things by themselves without "hand-holding", and through these opportunities, they seem to be more self-directed as learners. This can be seen in Finland's latest curriculum reform too. The new National Core Curriculum emphasizes developing student agency both inside and outside of school along with prioritizing the joy of learning and cultivating a collaborative learning environment. (Walker 2017, 93.)

Equally, Finnish schools have a lot of autonomy as well. Pokka (2015, 55) describes the Finnish school community as an autonomous operator at its best: *"Although guided by the national directives and the responsibilities assigned to it by the education provider, the school staff can themselves determine how they meet these goals."* The schools have the right to organize the teaching and learning according to their own administrative arrangements and visions, as long as the basic functions, determined by law, are carried out. Moreover, in many cases the budget management, acquisitions and recruitment are the responsibility of the schools. (Finnish Education in a Nutshell 2017, 12.)

One of the greatest tasks – and areas of autonomy – for Finnish schools is developing the local and school-specific curricula based on the National Core Curriculum. This development of a school-specific curriculum is a massive effort for the entire school community. It also allows the teaching staff to choose both the content of instruction and the methods with which that content will be taught. (Pokka 2015, 56.)

This autonomy also applies to education providers in general. Education providers, such as municipalities, schools, education institutions and so on, are responsible for practical teaching arrangements as well as the effectiveness and quality of their education. The regulations are loose when compared to

[4] Yes, there is homework in Finland, but it is fairly light when compared to other countries.

• • •

Finns simply do not think that competition is an effective way to promote learning.

• • •

many other countries; for example, there are no regulations for class sizes, and the education providers and schools are free to decide how to group pupils and students. (Finnish Education in a Nutshell 2017, 12.)

Collaboration

Finnish education is strikingly non-competitive when compared to other well-performing education systems in the world. There are no ranking practices for either students or teachers. Student performance is mostly compared to or contrasted with their own earlier achievements to see how their learning is proceeding.

Ari Pokka (2015, 24) notes that if one wants to see competition in Finnish school, it is the inner striving to do things as well as possible. Avoiding competition can be seen not only in the work of Finnish teachers and principals, but also in Finnish education politics and the discussion around it. This emphasis of discussion is based on the idea of human dignity and the equal value of each individual. Pokka sums it up well – top results, the names of successful students on marble plates or super teachers are not present in the narrative of the Finnish school. (Pokka 2015, 24; Walker 2017, 173.)

Where does this internationally unusual non-competitive emphasis stem from? Finns simply do not think that competition is an effective way to promote learning. Often when foreign visitors visit Finnish schools, they ask Finnish teachers that if they do not compare students to each other, how can they know who is the best student in the class? The answer of the Finnish teachers usually is "Why would I want to know that? Whose learning would it enhance?"

The only time Finnish teachers are interested in knowing who has performed "best" is when the annual grants and so called stipends (small sums of money) are awarded to pupils in the end of the school year. Still, the criteria for the stipends are varied: one might get it for the best report card GPA, but also for being the best and most motivated student in home economics or craft lessons, or for being the most friendly and well-behaving classmate. The stipends do not play a big role in Finnish education, but are rather seen as encouragement for good achievements, no matter what those achievements are.

Finnish teachers are always looking for additional means that would promote learning and well-being. Competition seems to enhance neither: competition is known to cause stress, fear and anxiety, which are all known to be an antidote to learning. In competitive situations, people tend to focus on being successful in achieving the predetermined learning outcomes rather than exploring new perspectives and unexpected results. In high-stake situations, students primarily learn alone rather than co-operatively with others in order to minimize personal risks. For teachers, the competition means minimizing risks, too. It means that open and alternative teaching methods and task designs are not favored because of their unpredicted results, and creativity in teaching declines. (Sahlberg 2006, 275.)

If Finns do not see competition as a driving force for better learning results, what is the key to better learning, then? For Finns it is co-operation. Pokka (2015, 10) points out that Finnish education professionals are strongly united by their shared ethos of the non-competitive school. Why is collaboration instead of competition seen as a better tool for enhancing learning? Pokka underlines that the strength of the non-competitive school is its ability to share its best practices with other schools and education professionals. This can be seen in the everyday encounters of principals and teachers where the best practices are shared without expectations of compensation. (Pokka 2015, 10.) Walker (2017, 173) sees "a culture of collaboration" in Finnish schools: *"Finnish teachers' non-competitive mind-set seems to help them work better together."* Pokka (2015, 10) states that in the end the winners of this collaborative and sharing school culture are Finnish children and adolescents who receive high-quality and constantly developing teaching. Walker describes this on-going collaboration among Finnish teachers:

> *In Finland, I found a school structure that fostered rich collaboration among teachers. In nearly 50 percent of my lessons, I was paired with one or two of my colleagues. Teachers in my school were not just collaborating in the traditional sense, by planning and teaching lessons together – they were truly laboring together, sharing the burdens of teaching with each other. They were helping each other track down resources they'd need for an upcoming lesson. They were discussing better ways to support needy students. They were analyzing the curriculum together. They were talking about how to improve recess for the kids. They were grading tests together. They*

were offering tech support to each other. To my surprise, this work often happened in between sips of coffee, during those fifteen-minute breaks throughout the day. (Walker 2017, 178–179.)

Walker makes several good remarks about the collaboration between teachers in Finland. Finnish teachers do not view collaboration as a luxury, but rather as a necessity in their work. Collaboration is not something structured or planned, it is something that happens organically – and often in the teachers' lounge. For Finnish teachers, collaboration is all about the mindset. (Walker 2017, 180–181.)

The collaborative atmosphere of Finnish schools can be seen in the students' way of working as well. In Finnish schools, teaching and learning methods vary considerably – there is traditional teacher-led teaching, independent studies and activating methods, but also a generous amount of project-based studies, different kinds of group work and co-operative learning methods, to name a few. The bottom line is that no matter what kind of teaching or learning, helping one's peers and learning from each other is not prohibited, but instead strongly encouraged in Finnish schools. Peer learning is considered a great resource and is constantly utilized in Finnish schools.

Working and learning with others is regarded as an important future skill for students in Finland. Sahlberg (2006, 271) states that social skills are necessary in productive group processes, whether it be at work or school. Collective intelligence, shared knowledge, team-based problem-solving, initiating and managing productive teamwork and continuous learning are viewed as key competencies for students in their future working life and life in general. (Sahlberg 2006, 271.) The new National Core Curriculum for Finnish Basic Education has the same emphasis (Finnish National Board of Education 2016).

Co-operation between schools is very common in Finland, as well. Pokka (2015, 121) notes that one of the strengths of Finnish schools is their willingness to collaborate both horizontally and vertically. The basis for this is the fact that Finnish schools have no reason to compete against each other. Since all schools are public and publicly funded and there are no school ranking lists, schools do not have to race against each other (see Pokka 2015, 24). Pokka also (2015, 121) suggests that the lack of competition between schools and the schools' ability to share positive experiences so that they can be turned into local or national development projects are behind the motivation to collaborate. *"Good ideas are not concealed but shared, free of charge, to be further developed by one's colleagues"* (Pokka 2015, 121).

This horizontal as well as vertical co-operation between Finnish schools and educational institutions is backed up by Finland's national education policy. On the other hand, the same widely used collaboration also guarantees that best innovations can become a part of the Finnish national education practices and policy as well. Pokka (2015, 123) points out that this kind of cooperation between schools and collegial dialogue has a substantial role in developing Finnish education politics. *"It guarantees that all the possible education professionalism that this small country contains is within the reach of each student and the development work is focused on refining good procedures into even better ones."* (Pokka 2015, 123.)

Collaboration between different schools and education institutions include joint development projects, sharing best practices, combining studies and creating a shared syllabus. This all demands a sense of strong trust and respect between schools, teachers and principals. It is a prerequisite for true collaboration that all parties have trust and respect for each other's skills and professionalism. (Pokka 2015, 123.) In addition to all this co-operation within the education community, collaboration is not restricted to occur within school buildings only. Finnish schools tend to co-operate with different partners and stakeholders: local communities, work places, other schools and educational institutions, various authorities, different non-profit organizations, libraries, museums, church and religious communities, international partners, media, parents and guardians etc. (Pokka 2015, 117–135).

The Finnish education community strongly believes that this multifaceted collaboration promotes the quality of education. International learning surveys seem to support this theory. Sahlberg (2007, 168) quotes Scheleicher's analysis of Finnish success: networks of schools that stimulate and spread innovations offer an explanation for Finland's success. This networking and collaborating also guarantees that all schools share a very similar quality in Finland; strong school performance is a consistent and predictable outcome throughout the education system, with less than 5% variation in student performance between different schools (Sahlberg 2007, 168). However, quality is not the only result of this co-operative approach. Hargreaves and Shirley (2008, 142) conclude that trust, co-operation, and responsibility create the collegiality and shared, committed, professional learning that improve classroom effectiveness and raise the standards of students in Finland.

The majority of education systems around the world seem to believe that education produces the best results when it is based on competition. Finland has chosen the opposite route. Pasi Sahlberg wraps up the Finnish mindset well:

> *I am offering a profound paradox: to prepare themselves for a more competitive economy, our schools and students must compete less. Schools should therefore increase internal collaboration against the external competition. Improving economic competitiveness requires well-educated and trained people, technological and network readiness and knowledge and skills to work in an innovation-rich world. Co-operation and networking rather than competition and disconnectedness should therefore lead the education policies and development of education systems. Schools and other educational institutions should cultivate attitudes, cultures and skills that are necessary in creative and collaborative learning environments.* (Sahlberg 2006, 285.)

Learner-centered

Finnish education is often seen as *"child-centered"* or *"student-centered"* (see e.g. Sahlberg 2017b, XIV; Walker 2017 60–68; Lonka 2018, 74–78). Education is not for the schools, teachers or parents – it is for the children and young people. The point of view from which Finns evaluate different changes or reforms in Finland is *"Is it beneficial for the children or young people?"* Pokka (2015, 31) states that the primary objective of the principal's work, for instance, goes beyond managerial or financial conditions; the main starting point is to do what is best for the students in the existing circumstances.

I have chosen to call Finnish schools *learner-centered* instead of child or student-centered for a particular reason. Namely, the concept "learner-centered" combines two key features in one term: it puts the person learning – the child, pupil or student – in the center, while it also emphasizes the priority of learning in Finnish education. The Finnish educational debate revolves around what kind of solutions or arrangements would promote learning the most. Learning is the key concept in Finnish education.[5] Teaching is discussed in relation to learning, such as what kind of teaching enhances learning the most. The aim of a school's work is to offer each student the learning environment and studying methods that best support

[5] Learning is not limited to acquiring new information. Learning is seen as an activity to look for new knowledge, skills and attitudes. Learning is about understanding the society and culture around you and seeing things in a wider, global context. Learning is about recognizing values and creating meanings. (Finnish National Board of Education 2016.)

their learning (see Pokka 2015, 31). A learner-centered school has *"students and their learning at its heart, and its aim is to provide the space and the possibility for learning"* (see Pokka 2015, 51).

Learner-centeredness means that students are considered to be true members and active agents of the school community. Their views are valued and their voices are heard. This student-centered approach offers new perspectives on organizing teaching, learning and other school operations. Pokka sees this as a basic value in Finnish education:

> *"One of the most fundamental starting points of any school value system is a respect for childhood and adolescence together with the recognition of the student's position as a fully pledged member of the school community."* (Pokka 2015, 24–25.)

• • •

Learner-centeredness means that students are considered to be true members and active agents of the school community.

• • •

What does it mean to be a learner-centered school? As stated earlier, to be truly learner-centered means that learners must be heard. The school must ask and allow the student's insights, both in critical feedback and in positive actions (Pokka 2015, 51). This requires comprehension, understanding how the young see the world. This also helps the school community react to cultural changes and new cultural phenomena. (Pokka 2015, 32.) However, being learner-centered does not mean that everything should be organized according to learners' wishes or that learners could dictate the school rules alone. Pokka clarifies that the student-centered approach is not the opposite of discipline. Everyone, including learners, must respect the learning community. A student-centered approach is thus a multi-lateral agreement between all those involved in the learning process, or the adults and children, to respect each other. (Pokka 2015, 51.) One of the defining qualities of the learner-centered approach is the focus on *well-being*. Well-being is both a prerequisite for learning and an intrinsic value in itself. Sahlberg (2017, XV) notes that in Finland, focusing on children's well-being, health and happiness in school has become one of the goals of schooling across the country. This can be seen especially in the New National Core Curriculum in which joy is prioritized as a learning concept (Walker 2017, 189). Well-being is seen as a promoter of learning as well. Walker refers to Adler stating that well-being and academic achievement are not antagonistic, as some have suggested. On the contrary, increased well-being improves learning and academic achievement. (Walker 2017, 188–189.)

Finnish education is often described as *stress-free*. One of the main reasons for the lack of stress is the lack of standardized tests. The only compulsory standardized test is the so-called matriculation examination (high school exit examination) which is usually taken at the age of 18 or 19. Sahlberg (2006, 282) concludes that the learning environment in Finnish schools is therefore safe and free from fear and anxiety, which are often caused by failing tests. The lack of stress is a component of well-being and thus a contributor of learning. Many other features of Finnish schooling also promote well-being: multiple daily recesses, short school days, long holidays, light homework and a relaxed atmosphere, just to name a few.

Science-based

Many of the above-mentioned characteristics of Finnish education – equality, trust, and co-operation – are highlighted in several publications. What is not often recognized is that Finnish education has a strong foundation in scientific research. Especially scientific studies on learning and educational psychology have guided the planning and implementation of Finnish education significantly.

The modern learning theory is the basis of Finnish teacher education and also the work of Finnish schools. The socio-constructivist learning theory has been well-represented in Finnish teacher education for years. Finnish teaching is largely based on the idea that knowledge and skills are attained through a learner's active construction, not only through direct instruction and accommodation. Learning is viewed a process that requires active participation, social interaction and reflection. (Lonka 2018, 28; Sahlberg 2006, 270.)

Many frequently used practices in Finnish schools are based on scientific research: recesses, light homework and physical activity are examples of this. Not only do they have a strong scientific basis, but Finnish teachers and students also experience their benefits in their everyday school work.

1. *Finnish schools have regular recesses.* Finland's Basic Education Decree sets a general regulation that provides all children with the right to

recess breaks in school. Usually there is a 15-minute break after every 45-minute lesson and one longer lunch break during the school day. Schools can also divide the breaks differently according to their own wishes. Pupils typically spend their recesses outside playing freely.

Scientific research has proved that recesses have several benefits. Recesses promote learning: spending some time outside the classroom during the school day in activities other than instruction can help improve students' performance in the classroom. Furthermore, breaks in instruction allow pupils to play, rest and freely interact with their peers to further develop their cognitive, emotional and social skills. Pupils can then apply those skills in the classroom, thus improving their learning. Children who have regular recesses during school days are more creative, more self-confident, less bullied and more attentive at school. (See Pellegrini et al. 2002; Pellegrini & Bohn 2005; OECD 2017, 336; Sahlberg 2017a, 19–20.)

2. Finnish schools are known to give a very *light amount of homework to pupils*. The general insight in Finland is that when the time at school is used efficiently for learning, there is no need to burden the children with an overload of homework in the evenings. Finnish teachers tend to emphasize quality over quantity when considering homework. If there is homework to be done at home, it should not be solely repetitive, but instead be beneficial to learning in some other way (application, expanding understanding and so on).

   There are scientific studies that support the fact that loads of homework do not promote learning. According to research, homework does not significantly improve academic achievement. The relationship between academic success and homework is minimal, if there even is one. On the contrary, loads of homework cause anxiety and stress which are known to hinder learning. Homework can also hurt students' attitudes toward school. (See Kralovec & Buell 2000; Kohn 2006; Shumaker 2016.)

3. *Increasing physical activity during the school day* is currently a huge trend in Finnish schools. This is stated in the New National Core Curriculum (Finnish National Board of Education 2016, 28). There is also a big national development program called *Finnish Schools on the Move* in Finland at the moment. The program aims to establish a

physically active culture in Finnish basic education and to ensure one hour of physical activity each day for all students. (Aira & Kämppi 2017.) A shared Finnish view is that increasing physical movement and integrating it into different school subjects promotes learning, academic achievement, health and general well-being of students. It is a common understanding in Finland that childrens' brains work better when children move.

There are numerous scientific studies stating that physical activity has a positive effect on learning and cognition. Scientific results demonstrate that physical movement can be an effective cognitive strategy to strengthen learning and enhance learner's motivation. In addition, physical activity has been found to have a positive effect on children's cognitive functions, such as memory, attention and general information processing and problem-solving skills. The scientific studies also indicate that increasing physical activity can improve test results, particularly in tasks requiring executive functions and memory. Furthermore, physical activity also appears to promote classroom behavior, concentration on assignments and participation in classwork. (See Donnelly et al. 2011; Kari et al. 2017; Jensen 2005; Rasberry et al. 2011; Reed et al. 2010; Sahlberg 2017a; Syväoja 2014; Syväoja 2015.)

Sahlberg (2007, 153) indicates that Finnish teacher education is prominently science-based. All basic education teachers must hold a Master's degree to be permanently employed. Teachers graduate from five-year university programs, and teaching is generally seen as a research-based profession in Finland. (Sahlberg 2007, 153.) Sahlberg summarizes the many effects this science-based approach has:

In international comparisons, Finnish teacher education programs are distinguished by their depth and scope --- The balance between the theoretical and practical in these programs helps young teachers master various teaching methods as well as the science of effective teaching and learning. --- teachers with high professional competency are quite motivated and easy to engage in school development processes in their own schools as well as in national and international projects. They also tend to work just as seriously at developing their own personal professional knowledge and skills. (Sahlberg 2007 154–155.)

Teaching is considered a research-based profession. Hannele Niemi (2016, 34) states that the goal of Finnish teacher education is to equip teachers with research-based knowledge and skills and methods for developing teaching. For the first, teachers need a deep knowledge of the most recent advances in research in the subjects they teach. For the second, they need to be familiar with the latest research concerning teaching and learning. Niemi concludes that it is the interdisciplinary research on subject content knowledge and pedagogical content knowledge that provides the foundation for developing teaching methods that can be adapted to suit different learners. (Niemi 2016, 34.) In addition, Lonka (2018, 30) emphasizes the importance of general pedagogical knowledge and educational psychology for teachers to efficiently promote learning.

Another subject of the research-based approach is the in-service training services for teachers. Finland has a strong emphasis on continuous upgrading of teachers' pedagogical skills and knowledge. Sahlberg (2007, 155) concludes that teaching profession in Finland is on a par with other professional careers; teachers can diagnose problems in their classrooms and schools, apply evidence-based solutions to them and evaluate and analyze the impact of implemented procedures. There is a similar kind of systematic and research-based way to prepare and continuously develop pedagogical leaders and to maintain their knowledge and skills in Finland (Sahlberg 2007, 167).

In conclusion

Finnish education is based on the above-mentioned cornerstones: equality and equity, trust and responsibility, autonomy, co-operation, learner-centeredness and research-based development. How these cornerstones are realized in different fields of Finnish education is further described in the following articles.

Teaching is considered a research-based profession.

References

Aira, A. & Kämppi, K. (Eds.) 2017. *Towards more active and pleasant school days.* Interim report on the Finnish Schools on the Move programme 2015–2016. LIKES Research Reports on Physical Activity and Health 335.

Donnelly J.E. & Lambourne K. 2011. Classroom-based physical activity, cognition, and academic achievement. *Preventive Medicine52*(1), 36–42.

Finnish Education in a Nutshell 2017. Education in Finland series. Finland's Ministry of Education and Culture and Finnish National Agency for Education. Accessed on 19 February 2020. Retrieved from_https://www.oph.fi/sites/default/files/documents/finnish_education_in_a_nutshell.pdf

Finnish National Board of Education 2016. *National core curriculum for basic education 2014.* Publications 2016:5. Helsinki.

Hargreaves, A. & Shirley, D. 2008. Beyond Standardization: Powerful New Principles for Improvement. *Phi Delta Kappan, 90*(2), 135–143.

Hargreaves, A. 2009. A decade of educational change and a defining moment of opportunity — an introduction. *Journal of Educational Change, 10*(2–3), 89–100.

Jensen, E. 2005. Teaching with the Brain in Mind. 2nd Edition. Aleksandria: Association for Supervision and Curriculum Development (ASCD).

Kari, J.T., Pehkonen, J., Hutri-Kähönen, N., Raitakari, O., & Tammelin T.H. 2017. Longitudinal associations between physical activity and educational outcomes. *Medicine and Science in Sports and Exercise, 49*(11), 2158–2166.

Kohn, A. 2006. *The Homework Myth: Why Our Kids Get Too Much of a Bad Thing.* Da Capo Press.

Kralovec, E. & Buell, J. 2000. *The End of Homework: How Homework Disrupts Families, Overburdens Children, and Limits Learning.* Boston: Beacon Press.

Lonka, K. 2018. *Phenomenal learning from Finland.* Helsinki: Edita.

Mullis, I.V.S., Martin, M.O., Foy, P., & Hooper, M. 2015. TIMSS (Trends in International Mathematics and Science Study) 2015 in Mathematics. IEA's TIMSS & PIRLS International Study Center, Lynch School of Education, Boston College. Niemi, H., Toom, A., & Kallioniemi, A. (Eds.) 2016. *Miracle of Education. The Principles and Practices of Teaching and Learning in Finnish Schools* (Second Revised Edition). Rotterdam: Sense Publishers.

Niemi, H. 2016. The Societal Factors Contributing to Education and Schooling in Finland. The Finnish Education: Equity and Quality as Its Main Objectives. In Niemi, H., Toom, A., & Kallioniemi, A. (Eds.) 2016. Miracle of Education. The Principles and Practices of Teaching and Learning in Finnish Schools (Second Revised Edition). Rotterdam: Sense Publishers, 23–40.

OECD 2016. *PISA 2015 Results (Volume I): Excellence and Equity in Education.* Paris: OECD Publishing.

OECD 2017. *Education at a Glance 2017: OECD Indicators.* Paris: OECD Publishing.

Pellegrini, A.D., Kato, K., Blatchford, P., & Baines, E. 2002. A Short-term Longitudinal Study of Children's Playground Games Across the First Year of School: Implications for Social Competence and Adjustment to School. *American Educational Research Journal, 39*(4), 991–1015.

Pellegrini, A. & Bohn-Gettler, C. 2005. The Role of Recess in Children's Cognitive Performance and School Adjustment. *Educational Researcher, 34*(1), 13–19.

Rasberry C.N., Lee S.M., Robin L., Laris B.A., Russell L.A., Coyle K.K., & Nihiser A.J. 2011. The association between school-based physical activity, including physical education, and academic performance: A systematic review of the literature. *Preventive Medicine52*(1), 10–20.

Reed, J.A., Einstein, G., Hahn, E., Hooker, S.P., Gross, V.P., & Kravitz, J. 2010. Examining the impact of integrating physical activity on fluid intelligence and academic performance in an elementary school setting: A preliminary investigation. *Journal of Physical Activity and Health7*, 343–351.

Pokka, A. 2015. *Top Class, Finnish School Leadership and Management*. Seinäjoki: Bookcover.

Sahlberg, P. 2006. Education reform for raising economic competitiveness. *Journal of Educational Change*, *7*(4), 259–287.

Sahlberg, P. 2007. Education policies for raising student learning: the Finnish approach. *Journal of Education Policy*, *22*(2), 147–171.

Sahlberg, P. 2015. *Finnish Lessons 2.0. What can the world learn from educational change in Finland?* Second edition. New York: Teachers College Press.

Sahlberg, P. 2017a. *FinnishED Leadership. Four ideas to improve schools*. Corwin Impact Leadership Series. Thousand Oaks: Corwin, A SAGE Company.

Sahlberg, P. 2017b. Foreword. In Walker, T. D. 2017. *Teach like Finland. 33 Simple Strategies for Joyful Classrooms*. New York: W.W. Norton & Company, XI–XIX.

Shumaker, H. 2016. *It's ok to go up the slide: Renegade rules for raising confident and creative kids.* New York: Tarcher.

Syväoja, H. 2014. *Physical activity and sedentary behaviour in association with academic performance and cognitive functions in school-aged children*. LIKES Research Reports on Sport and Health 292. University of Jyväskylä.

Syväoja, H. 2015. *Active body, active mind. How does physical activity affect learning?* LIKES – Research Center for Sport and Health Sciences / Finnish Schools on the Move programme.

Walker, T. D. 2017. *Teach like Finland. 33 Simple Strategies for Joyful Classrooms*. New York: W.W. Norton & Company.

2

THE NEW FINNISH NATIONAL CORE CURRICULUM: FROM WHY TO HOW

Päivi Valtonen (Lic.Ed.), Pedagogical Specialist, Learning Scoop, Tampere, Finland
Elena Chukhlantseva (M.Ed.), ECEC Specialist, Learning Scoop, Tampere, Finland

This chapter provides an overview of the path Finland has taken in formulating a new national core curriculum for basic education. The curriculum in a highly innovative policy document in ways it sets the stage for a transition to education of the 21st century. This chapter looks at why redefining the purpose of education is crucial in today's world of value-related questions, how renewed goals are translated into action and what we aim to achieve by doing so.

Curriculum reform in Finland

Finland changed the National core curriculum for basic education in 2014, and in August 2016[1] Finnish schools started implementing it. Many foreign experts have wondered why Finland changed the curriculum since Finland's previous curriculum brought excellent learning outcomes and results in international comparison (e.g. in OECD's Pisa tests). Why reform an obviously well-functioning system?

The world has changed tremendously since Finland's previous curriculum was released in 2004: there is the growing impact of globalization, challenges to sustainable future, new information, novel innovations, new problems and crises and so on. What brought Finland excellent learning results in the past does not necessarily meet the needs and challenges of the future.

[1] The new national core curriculum was actually released in 2014. The education providers, schools and teachers were given two years to internalize the goals of the new curriculum and to design how to put these guiding principles into practice in their own schools.

As Sahlberg (2015) states, the main purpose of the curriculum reform is not to reclaim the high test scores of previous years. The aim of the curriculum reform is to help teachers and educators teach what children and young people need in their lives. (Sahlberg 2015.) For years, the ultimate goal of Finnish education has been to prepare our children for life. We want our children to learn knowledge, skills, attitudes and values that will help in their life in the future. That is why we need to think, what are the key competences they will need in the rapidly changing world. What are the required skills for building a sustainable future? And what kind of practices would best produce the desired education and learning?

The key questions are: What do we see as the most important in the basic education right now? What have been the guiding principles in outlining the new national core curriculum? The guidelines for the new curriculum are based on Basic Education Act (628/1998):

- Growth towards humanity and responsible citizenship
- Necessary knowledge and skills
- Promoting education, equality and lifelong learning
- Sustainable future as an objective, global responsibility
- More participatory, physically active, creative and linguistically enriched schools
- Integrated teaching and learning.

The goal of the curriculum reform is pedagogical development. The new Finnish core curriculum can be discussed from three different perspectives, namely why, what and how:

- *Why* refers to the justification of the new approach. To put it shortly, we need a new approach in education, because the world has undergone major changes since the beginning of the 2000s. Especially the increasing impact of globalization and the challenges for a sustainable future require changes in education, too.

● ● ●

For years, the ultimate goal of Finnish education has been to prepare our children for life.

● ● ●

- *What* refers to the question of what the key knowledge, skills and competencies needed in society and working life are. The needs of society and working life have changed, especially when it comes to the required competencies. Building a sustainable future is one of the key competencies, and education needs to address this as well.
- It is not enough for us to know 'why' we need changes in education and 'what' types of knowledge and skills need to be secured. Therefore, the third vital question is: *How* should the content of teaching, pedagogy and school practices be reviewed and renewed in relation to the changes in the operating environment? (The Finnish National Board of Education 2014.)

The planning of a new curriculum in Finland is a long and thorough process. Unlike in many other countries, it is not a political process by nature, though. It involves various different stakeholders – teachers, authorities, researchers, parents, unions, education providers, educational professionals, a wide range of societal interest groups – but usually politicians do not take part in the designing of a new curriculum.

The new curriculum is research-based and has been carefully planned for over a decade. In fact, the curriculum reform can be seen as a national learning process for the whole community of educators and other professionals in the field, and as a learning cycle that helps identify the issues to be improved and promote the commitment of all stakeholders in the curriculum process. One of the most important stakeholder groups to play a key role in designing the new curriculum were the municipal education managers and teachers themselves. When professionals are part of the process, there is no need to use coercive power to implement the curriculum. (Lähdemäki 2019, 399–400.)

The new curriculum has been a "partnership-based and transparent planning process". This careful and interactive planning process has brought Finland and its educational community an open dialogue and a broad consensus over the new curriculum. (Halinen 2015; Vitikka, Krokfors & Rikabi 2016, 85.) In its process phase, the curriculum was subject to public discussion through three official commenting phases open for anyone interested to contribute with their views and opinions.

However, once the new curriculum was put into practice, an active discussion over it started among teachers and other parties involved: they were reflecting the pros and cons of the new curriculum and ways of implementing it in the best possible way. Even though the curriculum is revised quite seldom in Finland, there is a continuous development going on between the curriculum reforms, too.

The main ideas of the new Finnish national core curriculum

In the Finnish new national core curriculum are many interesting new perspectives to be explored. For this chapter, we have chosen the following aspects to be introduced in more detail:

- Transversal competences
- Multidisciplinary learning modules
- Phenomenon-based learning
- More versatile working methods
- Learning environments
- Increased physical activity
- Assessment as learning

Transversal competences support development as a human being and as a citizen

One of the main ideas of the Finland's new national core curriculum is the key competencies required in the future. These competences are broad or transversal by nature and they are not restricted to any particular school subjects. It is the task of every school subject to promote these competences.

The Finland's new National core curriculum for basic education (2016, 21) defines the transversal competences like this:

> *"Transversal competence refers to an entity consisting of knowledge, skills, values, attitudes and will. Competence also means an ability to apply knowledge and skills in a given situation. The manner in which the pupils will use their knowledge and skills is influenced by the values and attitudes they have adopted and their willingness to take action. The increased need for transversal competence arises from changes in surrounding world. Competences that cross the boundaries of and link different fields of knowledge and skills are a precondition for personal growth, studying, work and civic activity now and the future."*

The common objective of transversal competences is to support students' development as human beings and as citizens. Transversal competences encourage students to recognize their own uniqueness, personal strengths and development potential, and to appreciate themselves. (National core curriculum for basic education 2016, 21.)

The learning goals of the transversal competences are described as seven competence areas (National core curriculum for basic education 2016, 21–26):

- Thinking and learning to learn
- Cultural competence, interaction and self-expression
- Taking care of oneself and managing daily life
- Multiliteracy
- ICT competence
- Working life competence and entrepreneurship
- Participation, involvement and building a sustainable future

Local authorities and schools are encouraged to promote the development of these competences and to consider their own innovative ways in reaching the goals. The core curricula for subjects have been written so that learning objectives include the competence goals which are most important for the said objectives. The competences will also be assessed as a part of subject assessment. In this way, each school subject enhances the development of all seven competence areas. This is a new way of combining competence-based and subject-based teaching and learning. Nevertheless, the traditional school subjects will live on, though with less distinct borderlines and with more collaboration among them in practice.

In order to meet the challenges of the future, the focus is on transversal competences and work across school subjects. Collaborative classroom practices where pupils may work with several teachers simultaneously during periods of phenomenon-based project studies are emphasized.

One of the main goals of the new core curriculum for basic education is to create better opportunities for deep learning.

Multidisciplinary learning modules: work across school subjects

One of the main goals of the new core curriculum for basic education is to create better opportunities for deep learning. How can this be achieved? The proposed approach is to surpass the limits of individual subjects and emphasize cooperation among them by developing multidisciplinary learning modules. The use of multidisciplinary learning modules doesn't mean that teaching separate subjects is being abolished. The National core curriculum for basic education (2016, 32–33) contains important guidelines for the planning and implementation of multidisciplinary learning modules:

- Modules should help students connect knowledge and skills of different subjects, and organize their knowledge into large entities.
- Modules should be interesting and meaningful from the students' point of view.
- Teachers should plan and co-operate together.
- Students should participate in the planning and implementation of these modules.
- Students should be entitled to at least one integrative, multidisciplinary learning module every school year.

The detailed themes, contents and ways of executing the multidisciplinary learning modules are planned and decided at the local level, meaning in the local curriculum, in schools' annual plans and in co-operation between different subjects in schools (National core curriculum for basic education 2016, 33). The themes can be, for example, well-being, internationality, language and culture, life on the planet, my environment, nature, good habits and so on. The themes are usually broad and general. This yields the opportunity to implement themes in many ways in different subjects.

Phenomenon-based learning: towards deep learning and understanding

The new Finnish national core curriculum has a strong tendency to combine different school subjects. An example of this could be studying the same phenomena from different perspectives of different school subjects at the same time (National core curriculum for basic education 2016, 33). For instance, when studying the time Finland gained its independence in 1917, it is beneficial to understand the historical movements of the time (history) and how the societal changes of that time were reflected in the literature (Finnish language), art and music, instead of studying these things separately from each other at different points in time.

Combining the perspectives of different school subjects helps students understand phenomena better. In most cases, the phenomenon-based learning process begins with authentic and personal observations, experiences, and questions that interest learners. Phenomenon-based pedagogy is based on the idea that new knowledge and skills are built through modifying and extending previous knowledge and understanding. (Lonka, Hietajärvi, Hohti, Nuorteva, Rainio, Sandström, Vaara & Westling 2015, 51.) Phenomenon-based learning generates deep learning and personal insights. Phenomenon-based learning does not have to mean solving highly complex challenges like climate change and poverty, but rather everyday life situations that require an understanding of how different systems relate to each other (Lähdemäki 2019, 405).

The way how phenomenon-based learning is actually carried out may differ from school to school and in different cities. The local education providers (municipalities and cities), schools and teachers have a high degree of freedom in implementing nationally set objectives. They may develop their own innovative methods, which can differ from those in other municipalities or schools. (National core curriculum for basic education 2016, 33.)

More versatile working methods

The National core curriculum for basic education (2016, 31) emphasizes that teachers have to use more versatile, experiential and functional working methods. The starting point for the choice of working methods are the learning goals of the subjects along with the pupils' needs, abilities and interests (Reaching for the highest tree top 2016, 12).

The use of versatile working methods promotes students' awareness and understanding about a variety of individual and collaboratives ways to learn. It also enhances deeper learning, builds students' perception of themselves as learners and provides the teacher with diverse understanding of the students' performance.

It is not always the teacher who provides the information: students also learn how to search information, how to evaluate it and how to apply it to new situations. Students are encouraged to investigate and innovate things themselves, too, by using different learning methods and learning environments. Versatile methods bring the pupils joy of learning and experiences of success (National core curriculum for basic education 2016, 31). New modes of organizing teaching and learning contribute to students' engagement and motivation.

Learning environments

The learning environment has an essential role in Finnish education. The National core curriculum for basic education (2016) states that good learning environments support the growth, learning and interaction of the individual and the community. The objective is to develop learning environments that form a pedagogically versatile and flexible whole. (National core curriculum for basic education 2016, 30.)

The learning environment is defined as a specific learning setting, a physical environment, an indoor and outdoor space, and an operating practice where the educational process unfolds. The learning environment can be both the medium and the object of learning. Authentic real-life environments like libraries, museums, nature and science centers play an important part in Finnish education. Also, due to integration of technology and pedagogy, digital learning opportunities bring new elements and solutions along to the educational process. The use of various learning environments allows for more effective inclusion, differentiation and personalization of learning suited to the needs of different students.

The National core curriculum for basic education does not define what environments students should become acquainted with during compulsory basic education. As Salminen, Tornberg and Venäläinen (2016, 256) state, teachers in Finland are able to utilize different learning environments with the same independence as they have when teaching within their classrooms. The only basic requirements to observe when choosing, designing and using various learning environments are safety, the holistic well-being of students and fitness for educational purposes.

Increased physical activity

The positive effects of exercise on the health of children are undeniable. Studies have shown that physical activity during school days is an effective way of improving the physical fitness of children and preventing disorders such as cardiovascular diseases. Good physical fitness and functional ability are important not only for health but also for learning. Studies have examined the effects of physical activity during school day on school achievement.

Physical activity during school days and good stamina in specific have a positive impact on school grades. (Syväoja, Kantomaa, Laine, Jaakkola, Pyhältö & Tammelin 2012, 13, 24.)

School is a place that reaches the whole age group: it offers an excellent framework for increasing the physical activity of children. Various options for increasing the physical activity of children are available in the school. Physical education constitutes an important basis for physical activity. In addition to this, the 15 to 30 minutes recesses between lessons, use of functional working methods during lessons, various sport events and projects (such as the Finnish Schools on the Move program[2]) increase physical activity during the school day and help in adopting a healthy lifestyle. (Syväoja, Kantomaa, Laine, Jaakkola, Pyhältö & Tammelin 2012, 27–28.) In Finland, it is also quite normal for children to walk or cycle several kilometers to and from school. These trips between home and school are, for many children, an important part of physical exercise during the day.

Physical activity has a significant role in the national curriculum for basic education in Finland. The schools which have been involved in the Move program for a few years already have been implementing the elements of the new national curriculum in their every-day school life. (Haapala 2017, 61.)

Assessment as learning

In Finland, the task of assessment is to support, guide and encourage students, and to promote learning. The school helps students learn to analyze and understand their own learning processes and take more responsibility over their own learning. (Halinen 2015.) The assessment focuses on the student's learning, working skills and behavior. The students and their achievements and successes are not compared to each other. The assessment shall never focus on the student's personality or their personal characteristics. (National core curriculum for basic education 2016, 50–51.)

---

[2] Finnish Schools on the Move is a national action program aiming to establish a physically active culture in Finnish comprehensive schools. Schools and municipalities participating in the program implement their own individual plans to increase physical activity during the school day. The Schools on the Move program is carried out by the Finnish National Board of Education and the Ministry of Education and Culture. The program is financed with lottery funding and coordinated by the LIKES Research Centre for Sport and Health Sciences. Finnish Schools on the Move program started with a pilot phase (2010–2012). In May 2017, more than 90% of municipalities and 80% of comprehensive schools (2000 schools) were involved in the program. (Finnish Schools on the Move program, https://liikkuvakoulu.fi/english 8.2.2018)

A reliable assessment requires versatile and flexible assessment practices that go beyond accountability and have a process orientation. The teacher gathers information on the student's progress in various areas of learning and in different learning situations. (National core curriculum for basic education 2016, 50–51.) The teacher's assessment is coupled with the student's self-assessment. To develop the pupils' capabilities to use self-assessment is an important task of basic education (Finnish education in a nutshell 2017, 17).

Self-assessment may concern individual students or peer groups engaged in joint work. In lower grades, self-assessment skills are developed by helping students notice and understand their own successes and strengths in school work. In higher grades, it is still important to recognize successes and strengths, but the reflection of the student's learning and progress is more analytic. (National core curriculum for basic education 2016, 51.) Self-assessment allows the students to have control or ownership of their learning and guides them to develop a sense of responsibility and self-motivation. The students continuously review their learning progress as individuals or as a group and practice to self-direct their learning by setting goals and planning how to meet those goals. In this way, students become more and more self-regulated.

A good assessment culture implies an open interaction and constructive feedback flow between the teacher and the student, and co-operation between home and school. For teachers, assessment is also an instrument of self-assessment and means reflecting on their own work. (National core curriculum for basic education 2016, 49.)

Tips for all teachers

Teachers cannot reform the educational system of their country by themselves. However, every teacher can adopt Finnish ways of teaching and acting to make their students learn better and more easily. We would like to propose a few ideas based on the new Finnish curriculum for basic education that any teacher can use.

Every teacher can adopt Finnish ways of teaching and acting to make their students learn better and more easily.

"Each pupil is unique and valuable just as he or she is" (National core curriculum for basic education 2016, 15). The foundation for all educational activities is the respect, appreciation and caring of the child. Each student needs encouragement and individual support in their personal growth and learning. The positive pedagogy is an excellent tool for all teachers. The aim of positive pedagogy is to prevent and to facilitate. The prevention means that students should be provided with what it takes to improve their resilience and their power to remain intact and to be capable to recover when faced by crises in life. The facilitation means that the school is like a treasury of positive interaction and growth in being human; the purpose is to promote the holistic development of individuals. Receiving encouraging feedback, finding one's own strengths and learning to work persistently and enjoying it opens up a positive development path far into the future. (Uusitalo-Malmivaara & Vuorinen 2017, 10.)

"Learning takes place in interaction with other pupils." Learning together promotes the students' skills in creative and critical thinking and problem-solving and students' ability to understand different viewpoints. (National core curriculum for basic education 2016, 17.) Interaction skills can be practiced. The teacher can enhance interaction in the classroom by using versatile working methods. Cooperative methods, for example, are suitable for increasing interaction. Students learn to work together and the teacher learns to guide the group work and interaction.

"Close cooperation among the staff facilitates the implementation of the school's educational goals" (National core curriculum for basic education 2016, 38). Co-operation between adults works as a great example for the students. At its best, the whole school operates as a learning community. Close co-operation among teachers of different subjects also promotes learning: students get a good overall understanding of the studied theme or subject, and they have a chance to organize their knowledge into large entities, which in turn will make deep learning possible (cf. multidisciplinary learning modules).

"The pupils' involvement in planning their own school work and their group's activities is a natural way of reinforcing participation" (National core curriculum for basic education 2016, 37). Students should be heard. They should be given the opportunities to share their thoughts and ideas regarding school work and their own learning. Children should also be given the opportunity to influence, even to a small extent, their own learning and learning environments. Observing children is also important. Teachers and educational assistants should observe the children and reflect on what they need for learning, what

is best for them. This is an important part of the student-centered approach in learning.

"A learning community understands the importance of physical activity for learning and diminishes a sedentary way of living" (National core curriculum for basic education 2016, 27). Students will move more when they are given the opportunity to move. There are different options for increasing the physical activity of students during the school day: the recesses, short physical activity breaks during the lessons, functional and activating working methods in the classroom, and sport events like sports days.

References

Finland 628/1998. Basic Education Act 21.8.1998. Helsinki: National Board of Education. Available at: https://www.finlex.fi/fi/laki/kaannokset/1998/en19980628.pdf

Cantell, H. (Ed.) 2015. *Näin rakennat monialaisia oppimiskokonaisuuksia* [How to build multidisciplinary learning modules]. Jyväskylä: PS-kustannus.

Finnish Education in a Nutshell 2017. The Ministry of Education and Culture and the Finnish National Agency for Education. Brochure.

The Finnish National Board of Education (FNBE). 2014. Irmeli Halinen: General Aspects of Basic Education Curriculum Reform 2016 Finland. Retrieved 5 October 2016 from www.youtube.com/watch?time_continue=7&v=KY_LZJkEo28

Finnish Schools on the Move programme. https://liikkuvakoulu.fi/english 8.2.2018

Halinen, Irmeli 2015. What is going on in Finland? – Curriculum Reform 2016. Blog text 25.3.2015. http://oph.fi/english/current_issues/101/0/what_is_going_on_in_finland_curriculum_reform_2016 8.2.2018

Haapala, H. 2017. *Finnish schools on the Move: Students' physical activity and school-related social factors.* LIKES Research Reports on Physical Activity and Health 336. University of Jyväskylä. Faculty of Sport and Health Sciences. Sport Pedagogy and Social Sciences of Sport. Jyväskylä: University Printing House.

Juuti, K., Kairavuori, S., & Tani, S. 2015. Tiedonalalähtöinen eheyttäminen [Discipline-based integration]. In Cantell, H. (Ed.) *Näin rakennat monialaisia oppimiskokonaisuuksia* [How to build multidisciplinary learning modules]. Jyväskylä: PS-kustannus, 77–92.

Lonka, K., Hietajärvi, L., Hohti, R., Nuorteva, M., Rainio A. P., Sandström, N., Vaara, L., & Westling, S. K. 2015. Ilmiölähtöisesti kohti innostavaa oppimista [Towards inspiring learning with the help of a phenomenon]. In Cantell, H. (Ed.) *Näin rakennat monialaisia oppimiskokonaisuuksia* [How to build multidisciplinary learning modules]. Jyväskylä: PS-kustannus, 49–72.

Lähdemäki, J. 2019. Case study: The Finnish national curriculum 2016—A co-created national educational policy. In: Cook Justin W. (ed) 2019. Sustainability, human well-being and the future of education. Palgrave Macmillan: Cham, Switzerland, 397–422. Downloaded at https://www.palgrave.com/gp/book/9783319785790

National core curriculum for basic education 2014 2016. Finnish National Board of Education. Publications 5. Helsinki.

Reaching for the highest tree top 2016. Kangasala pre-primary and basic education and the Finnish Core Curriculum.

Sahlberg, P. 2015. *Finland's school reforms won't scrap subjects altogether.* The Conversation. http://theconversation.com/finlands-school-reforms-wont-scrap-subjects-altogether-39328

Salminen, J., Tornberg, L., & Venäläinen, P. 2016. Public institutions as learning environments in Finland. In Niemi, H., Toom, A., & Kallioniemi, A. (Eds) *Miracle of Education. The Principles and Practices of Teaching and Learning in Finnish Schools.* Rotterdam: Sense Publishers, 253–266.

Syväoja, H., Kantomaa, M., Laine, K., Jaakkola, T., Pyhältö, K., & Tammelin, T. 2012. *Liikunta ja oppiminen* [Movement and learning]. Opetushallituksen tilannekatsaus [Review by the Finnish National Board of Education]. Muistiot [Notes] 5. Helsinki: Opetushallitus [Finnish National Board of Education].

Uusitalo-Malmivaara, L., & Vuorinen, K. 2017. *Huomaa hyvä! Näin ohjaat lasta ja nuorta löytämään luonteenvahvuutensa* [See the good! How to guide children and youth in finding their character strengths]. Jyväskylä: PS-Kustannus.

Vitikka, E., Krokfors, L., & Rikabi, L. 2016. The Finnish National Core Curriculum. Design and Development. In Niemi, H., Toom, A., & Kallioniemi, A. (Eds) *Miracle of Education. The Principles and Practices of Teaching and Learning in Finnish Schools.* Rotterdam: Sense Publishers, 83–90.

2.1

DESIGNING LESSONS IN FINLAND

Johanna Järvinen-Taubert (M.Ed.), Pedagogical Director, Learning Scoop, Tampere, Finland
Päivi Valtonen (Lic.Ed.), Pedagogical Specialist, Learning Scoop, Tampere, Finland

Lesson planning plays a major role in teaching in Finland. All lessons should be based on the national core curriculum and promote the learning goals described in the curriculum.

Designing lessons and larger learning modules beforehand helps create meaningful learning situations and achieve better learning results. The teacher can always be flexible and change plans during the lesson but planning lessons in advance is helpful for building further developed and more beneficial lessons for students.

Designing quality lessons is in the very core of Finnish teacher training. During teacher training, teacher students in Finland are taught different options and possibilities of how to design lessons in a pedagogically productive way. During their studies, teacher students plan several lessons and get feedback on their lesson plans. After reviewing their plan, they execute their planned lessons in practice, get feedback from their teacher trainers and peer students and reflect on their experiences in order to improve their expertise in this field.

• • •

Designing lessons and larger learning modules beforehand helps create meaningful learning situations and achieve better learning results.

• • •

The purpose of beforehand planning is to enhance learning the best possible way. That is why planning is based on the latest scientific research on learning and how it can be fostered as effectively as possible. It is vital that teachers-to-be acquire a strong foundation of what learning is and how it can be promoted. Another essential factor is getting a versatile "toolbox" of different methods and pedagogical practices for choosing the most suitable pedagogical solution for different groups and situations. (Lonka 2018; Sahlberg 2015.)

The socio-constructivist view on learning

Modern educational research has revealed many factors that promote learning: learner's own activity, motivation, participation, collaborative learning (learning with and from each other), reflection, connections to prior knowledge, physical activity, using versatile methods etc. This contemporary learning theory that has been the basis for teaching and lesson planning in Finland for years is called the socio-constructivist view of learning. (Lonka 2018, 28–48.)

The socio-constructivist view of learning rests on the following principles:

- Learning is perceived as an active, not passive, process through which knowledge is constructed by the learner.
- Knowledge is mutually built and constructed in the social contexts of learning.
- Prior knowledge, understanding and experiences are relevant to learning new things.
- The teacher's role is to support and nurture the learning process: teachers are facilitators who enable students' development and learning. (Lonka 2018, 28.)

Finnish teachers base their work on the socio-constructivist view and apply it daily in various ways. The approach can manifest in many diverse ways in the classroom:

- engaging learners in activity, discourse, and reflection
- frequent use of discussions and participation
- giving learners an opportunity to present their own questions and construct their own models
- encouraging independent thinking: students test their ideas, synthesize the ideas of others, build a deeper understanding of what they are learning and develop reasoning skills

- using various activating and co-operative teaching methods. (Lonka 2018, 50–57; Walker 2017.)

The socio-constructivist approach to learning not only produces excellent learning results but also promotes the acquisition of useful skills for life. The approach encourages learners to be active in constructing their own knowledge and to collaborate to solve problems together with other learners. It fosters important life skills such as self-regulation, self-determination and perseverance. The approach also promotes collaborative skills such as respectful communication, negotiating, compromising, tolerance, ability to encourage one's teammates, appreciation of diversity, working constructively with different types of people and so on. These life skills, especially analytic reasoning, complex problem solving and teamwork are a prerequisite for deeper learning.

Students' well-being can be increased by promoting their own activity, participation and involvement. Student well-being is as important as the learning outcomes. A stress-free and engaging atmosphere in the classroom promotes learning and enhances the general well-being of the children, young people and teachers alike. It is possible to achieve excellent learning results and feel joy over learning simultaneously (Walker 2017, xxvii-xxix).

How to design a lesson?

Usually the process of designing a lesson contains the following steps:

- Recognizing the preconditions
- Setting the learning goals
- Choosing the contents
- Deciding the structure of the lesson and the teaching methods
- Determining the assignments
- Setting the lesson's timetable
- Planning the needed resources

There is not one right order for following these steps. Many steps can even be considered simultaneously. To keep up the on-going improvement of one's lessons, the planning cycle should also include:

- Putting the lesson plan into practice
- Reflecting on the experiences and targets for improvement after the lesson

All this is very standard thinking in Finland. It is a regular practice for Finnish teachers to plan their lessons in advance and reflect on their experiences afterwards. Nevertheless, the methods of doing this may vary. Some Finnish teachers write their detailed plans down, whereas others have "internalized" this planning cycle and therefore do not necessarily make a myriad of notes.

How to plan quality lessons the Finnish way?

Finnish education experts created a mobile app to model the Finnish way of planning lessons. This app is called LessonApp, and it is an application that helps teachers plan versatile and high-quality lessons. It is based on the socio-constructivist view of learning and follows a Finnish lesson designing process.

LessonApp is a tool with 'building blocks' which the teachers can use to plan versatile and purposeful lessons. The building blocks are divided into five categories according to the key elements of the socio-constructivist view on learning:

1. Warm-up and grouping/safe atmosphere for learning
2. Orientation and mapping pre-existing knowledge/what learners already know about the matter
3. Acquiring new information/constructing one's own knowledge
4. Practicing/learners being active themselves
5. Reflection/learners deepening their learning via conscious thinking processes

Each building block represents a phase or a function of a lesson. The idea is to construct lessons by using these blocks according to the goal of the lesson: not all blocks are necessary in each lesson, and their order can vary depending on the purpose and objective of the lesson. You can find more information on www.lessonapp.fi.

References

Lonka, K. 2018. *Phenomenal learning from Finland*. Helsinki: Edita.

Sahlberg, P. 2015. *Finnish lessons 2.0. What can the world learn from educational change in Finland?* New York: Teachers College Press.

Walker, T. 2017. *Teach like Finland. 33 Simple strategies for joyful classrooms*. New York: W.W. Norton & Company.

2.2

ACTIVATING METHODS IN CLASSROOM

Kaisa Tuomarla (M.Ed.), Class teacher, Atala primary school (grades K-6), Tampere, Finland

"Versatile working methods bring the pupils joy of learning and experiences of success and support creative activities characteristic of different age groups. Experiential and functional working methods, the engagement of different senses and the use of movement increase the experiential nature of learning and strengthen motivation."
Finnish National Board of Education 2016, 31

A teacher stands in the front of the classroom and talks. Students are listening, maybe taking notes. After the lecture, students write in their notebooks and fill out exercises. Sounds familiar?

This model of teaching, where a teacher pours information and pupil's role is just to listen and sit still, is a traditional school method. Sometimes there is a need for this model as well, but if it is the only teaching method in the class, all skills in learning, socializing, collaborating will remain narrow.

Let us think about the modern society and its requirements of an individual's skills in working life. How does the traditional teaching method support the future skills? Let us now imagine a situation: a person goes to a job interview and is asked "What are you good at?" Will they answer: "I am very good at listening and sitting still"?

Society and working life require people to be skilled in negotiating, collaborating and learning. These skills develop through the person's life, starting in childhood. It is important that these skills are practiced at school as well.

Additionally, research shows that activating learning methods are a more effective way of learning. Activating methods increase the pupil's involvement, motivation and attention, and also develop certain cognitive aspects better than traditional teaching. Activating methods develop skills in analysis, synthesis and evaluation. They also increase helpfulness, empathy and other social skills.

The Finnish National core curriculum for basic education emphasizes that teachers should use more versatile, experimental, functional and activating methods. In Finland, teachers have the power to decide which methods they use in their lessons.

Activating methods form a wide spectrum of different methods. However, in these different methods, certain common principles are fulfilled: activation, learning through experiences, utilization of the group, interaction and creativity. The starting point for the choice of methods are the learning goals of the subjects and the pupils' needs, abilities and interests.

Students of different ages need different methods. Even the pre-primaries benefit from activating methods, and it is very important to start early: variation in methods creates a rich learning environment. The traditional teaching is only one part of it, but it still has an important role in creating peace and safety in classroom.

The first small step is to activate a traditional lesson. A notebook lesson can be activated with small plays, games and discussions. Sometimes the activating method is about creating small "buzz groups". Students' discussions and conversations create new information, assess prior knowledge and solve tasks. For me, LessonApp – a Finnish mobile app for designing lessons – is a database of all my favorite activating methods. LessonApp offers many ways to use these methods in different subjects with various age groups.

The co-operative learning is one of my favorite methods. Students work in teams of four or five, and every student has been given a role: a leader, a secretary, an observer, an encourager or an organizer. The roles and tasks

Activating methods increase the pupil's involvement, motivation and attention, and also develop certain cognitive aspects better than traditional teaching.

will be explained and learned, after which the team works together. The co-operational learning team can be used in everyday situations. For example, the leader is the one who takes care of leading their team outdoors or to wash hands. The teams work together with given topic during the lessons. The roles change every day so that everyone has a chance to try each role. This method is excellent with every age group, from pre-primaries to adults. Believe me, this has been tested!

Moreover, activating methods make teachers abandon the notebooks: they are not always relevant in learning and assimilating information. New things can be studied in learning labs and workshops. New digital environments assist in learning? and enable the teacher to be a supportive mentor instead of an information pouring character. New learning environments can also be found in school hallways, gym halls and especially outdoors.

School hunt is one of the methods for young students outside the classroom. It merges treasure hunting with learning and walking: students walk around the school hunting for words, numbers or forms. It can be used in math, languages, science, history, religion and other subjects. Detailed instructions for the method can be found in LessonApp.

Buzz groups and school hunts are good examples of easy, quick methods. They add inspiration and participation to students' learning in a short time: buzz groups last only certain part of a lesson, whereas school hunt takes 1–2 lessons. An example of a long-term activating method would be project-based learning. The teacher's role is to create the topic and the schedule, give information, and offer guidance and support during the project. The project could be a research made by pairs or teams, a portfolio or a poster. It could also be a project called "design you own school week", where the teacher gives topics and subjects of the week and students' learning teams decide how they are going to address the week's topics. The project's duration can vary: it can last only one day, or be used during history lessons during one month, or it can last several months, taking few hours every week.

It is good to remember that not all methods are good in every classroom. The self-imposed learning and projects can be very difficult for a child who has problems with directing attention and self-control, for example, since they usually need very structural routines. They may have to struggle excessively with long-term, unprompted projects. Remember, professional-made notebooks do have their place! Small activating methods like buzz groups suit everyone, and the co-operative learning method with given roles also surprisingly helps kids with special needs participate.

Learning by doing is an old way of teaching, this wheel was invented long time ago. Researchers have studied this for decades: a human being learns more, deeper and better, if they can participate and be active in their own learning.

Reference

Finnish National Board of Education 2016. *National core curriculum for basic education 2014*. Publications 2016:5. Helsinki.

2.3

PHENOMENON-BASED LEARNING IN FINNISH EDUCATION

Johanna Järvinen-Taubert (M.Ed.), Pedagogical Director, Learning Scoop, Tampere, Finland
Elena Chukhlantseva (M.Ed.), ECEC Specialist, Learning Scoop, Tampere, Finland

Phenomenon-based learning is a part of Finland's latest national core curricula for education of all levels from early childhood to upper secondary education (K-12), including basic education.

The goal of phenomenon-based learning is for students to explore various real-life phenomena from different perspectives. Phenomenon-based learning as implemented in Finland does not aim to abandon school subjects, but rather add new multidisciplinary study units for all students at different levels of education. Such multidisciplinary units promote establishing connections across a range of subjects and develop a more holistic understanding of the world around us.

However, the concepts of multidisciplinary studies and phenomenon-based learning have a slightly different emphasis. By *multidisciplinary studies* we usually refer to the fact that each school year, every school in Finland must have at least one clearly defined theme, project or course that combines the content of different subjects and deals with the selected theme from the perspective of several subjects. *Phenomenon-based learning*, on the other hand,

The goal of phenomenon-based learning is for students to explore various real-life phenomena from different perspectives.

implies that holistic real-world phenomena are studied as complete entities in their real context from different perspectives (of different school subjects) at the same time. In phenomenon-based learning, the phenomenon itself is both the starting point and object of studying and learning.

Both multidisciplinary and phenomenon-based learning seek to open the door to a coherent view of the world, which is then gradually expanded and structured. New perspectives, concepts, values, and attitudes as well as new knowledge and skills are built and enhanced through a) co-planning of the learning objectives, learning environments and activities, b) co-implementing, and c) co-assessing of the process and outcomes. Versatile working approaches bring teaching methods and learning methods together. They are the both the objects of learning and learning tools at the same time (e.g. group work, outdoor learning, digital devices).

The themes for multidisciplinary study units and phenomenon-based learning are formulated according to the curriculum, students' age, interesting current topics and sometimes students' own interests also. Here are some examples:

- Me and my community, Books are my friends (ECEC, 3–5 years)
- Wonders of the forest, Space (pre-primary, 6 years)
- What it was like in the old days in our own home town (1st graders, 7 years)
- Finland's 100th anniversary, Well-being, Global world (1st–6th graders, 7–12 years)
- Stories in our world (3rd–6th graders, 9–12 years)
- Olympic games (4th graders, 10 years)
- Sustainable development, recycling (5th–6th graders, 11–12 years)
- Sustainable living and circular economy (7th graders, 13 years)
- Climate change (7th–9th graders, 13–15 years)
- World of energy (8th and 9th graders, 14–15 years)
- Democracy in today's world (1st and 2nd graders in general upper secondary school, 16–17 years).

The themes of the multidisciplinary study units can be decided by the municipality (city), school, group of teachers or individual teachers. Sometimes the student union can decide the theme for multidisciplinary studies; sometimes the students of one class suggest a topic they would like to investigate closer.

Since schools and teachers have a high autonomy in Finland, there are multiple ways of organizing these multidisciplinary study units. Here are only a couple of examples of the different models:

1. The school has a special week for multidisciplinary studies. During this week, students do not have regular lessons, but instead they work in small groups and participate in different workshops conducted by different teachers that cover different aspects of the theme.
2. The school has a monthly theme day related to the chosen theme of the multidisciplinary studies. During these days, students from different grades work in mixed small groups and participate in different workshops all related to the chosen theme.
3. Every grade level has their own multidisciplinary study unit and theme. Several (or all) subject teachers for that grade plan together how to integrate their own teaching into the theme and other subjects. Teachers plan flexible solutions, how to create mutual tasks that require application of different subject-related knowledge, skills and methods. Additionally, they combine lessons and co-teach when possible and so on.
4. Different classes can have different projects that require skills and knowledge of various different school subjects. The theme of the project can be decided by or together with the students. Teachers facilitate the project by integrating different school subjects to the theme and project whenever needed.
5. Students select the topic they want to study closer. The teacher facilitates the process by providing different resources from different knowledge areas and school subjects every time new questions arise. The process is very organic, student-led, and has no pre-set learning goals other than understanding and exploring the chosen phenomenon.

During these phenomenon-based or multidisciplinary study units, some teachers use learning diaries to enhance coherent information creation, reflection and self-assessment.

Design and implementation of multidisciplinary study units and phenomenon-based learning require co-operation between the teachers and educators working in the same team, in the same grade level, and/or across different subjects. Multidisciplinary and phenomenon-based learning should rely on certain guidelines and supportive structures. Well-balanced educational process is goal-oriented but not goal-dominated. It focuses on the future, but not at the expense of reducing the importance of the present to the learner. Too many open opportunities within learning modules may result in losing focus or leaving things undone, or drifting into chaos.

The need for multidisciplinary studies as well as phenomenon-based learning starts with the same remark: in order to understand the world around us, it is essential to study the complexity of real-life phenomena. Furthermore, if we want to gain the skills needed in real life, we must practice them in actual problem-solving situations.

The whole idea of strengthening the multidisciplinary approach in Finnish education has been to learn the vital *skills needed in the future*. These skills are called transversal competencies, and they play a central role in the Finnish National core curriculum for basic education. These transversal competencies should be applied to all learning areas and school subjects.

This holistic approach has raised a lot of international interest. Professor Kirsti Lonka from the University of Helsinki published an in-depth book about the topic: Phenomenal Learning from Finland (2018).

In her book, Professor Lonka clearly states the need for this kind of wider approach: *"[T]he society is changing so rapidly that creativity, thinking skills, and more wide-ranging expertise are called for. --- Holistic and interdisciplinary thinking is important when solving the ill-structured and wicked problems of our time."* (Lonka 2018, 174–175.)

It is of paramount importance for students to learn to acquire information, tools, strategies and capabilities by means of which they are able to gradually increase their ability to examine, experience and understand various phenomena. Phenomenon-based learning empowers students to take ownership of their learning through active participation, diversification of learning objectives, working approaches and ways of assessment.

In the end, the most important thing of phenomenon-based learning might not be the holistic understanding students gain about important issues as such. It is the journey that is meaningful: *"In high-quality and meaningful learning, we can make use of the human readiness to wonder, investigate, and go beyond personal ideas in intensive group work. --- Developing high-quality thinking needs space for inquiries and wondering, even though it occurs within formal schooling."* (Lonka 2018, 178.)

Reference

Lonka, K. 2018. *Phenomenal learning from Finland.* Helsinki: Edita.

2.4

STEAM ENABLES CROSS-CURRICULUM WORK AND CO-OPERATION BETWEEN TEACHERS

Jukka Miettunen (M.Ed.), Principal, Yli-Ii comprehensive school (grades K–9), Oulu, Finland

I work as the Principal of the Yli-Ii Comprehensive School in the City of Oulu. Our school has put a lot of effort into STEAM. STEAM, which means Science Technology Engineering Arts and Mathematics, is a rising star amongst trends in education.

Four years ago, my school started a transformation towards a 21st Century School, enabling students to train their future skills such as creativity, critical thinking, problem-solving and use of technology. Because we are in Finland, students are of course our focus area number one; the other goal was to help teachers engage in more co-operation and combine their strengths.

In Finland, we have a new curriculum promoting transversal competences and cross-curricular themes that enables co-operation between subjects. Co-operation is a skill that every Finnish teacher has to learn and start to utilize in their own work. It also requires innovative initiatives and strong leadership from the school leaders to guide the school into the right direction in the changing world. What a great opportunity to have STEAM as a framework to combine subjects and teachers!

For primary teachers (grades 1–6), who teach most of the subjects by themselves, working cross-curricularly is often smooth. This however is not the case for secondary school teachers, who normally teach two or three subjects. It is challenging for a principal to organize timetables so that subject teachers could co-operate. Collaboration of secondary school teachers was one of the challenges we started to tackle.

At first, we had some benchmarking to do. We heard that Danish schools have FabLabs (Fabrication Laboratory) at schools. FabLabs are equipped with modern STEAM tools like 3D printers, laser cutters, vinyl cutters and robotics, and they have developed a pedagogical model and design model to utilize those. We decided to have something like that in our school, too. We wanted to have a STEAM Learning Environment serving all the students at the school, helping teachers co-operate between STEAM subjects and supporting professional development in the changing world.

We built up a STEAM Learning Environment called STEAMario (Värkkäämö in Finnish). It means making something in a strong sense of "doer culture" that has been a vital skill during hard times here in Finland after II World War. We also trained our teachers to use it and its technology easily. Today, STEAMario is a modern and stimulating STEAM Learning Environment with necessary technology like coding, robotics, electric work, laser cutting and carving, and vinyl printing.

To support the development phase, we also established a STEAM team with teachers interested and willing to learn new skills. Now we have an environment and a working culture that is well known here in Finland and abroad too. We have had several visitors having workshops or just benchmarking us. The impact for the whole community has been tremendous!

Most of the projects and prototypes done in STEAMario rise from the real world problem-solving. For example, we had an Autumn holiday for a week. Students had just planted seeds to grow chili in biology class. They were worried that the plant will dry without watering during the week. With some planning together, they created an automatic watering system controlled by Arduino. Well-watered chilis were awaiting the students after the holiday week.

In another project, students were examining everyday automation and finding ideas to solve their own problems. They watched a video of a Finnish inventor who talked about how he views automation, how he ended up as an inventor and how he feels about the importance of creativity. The final projects represented problem-solving for things like cleaning your room – a cleaning robot making your bed – a bed making tool and so on. What a joy of learning and doing things together!

Learning is the most important goal, and pedagogy plays a major role in the planning and executing STEAM-projects. With STEAM, the students have more opportunities to train their skills and find their strengths. There are success stories especially with students who have a lack of motivation: the most eager STEAM Learning Environment users are students of the JOPO class (Flexible Basic Education). The JOPO class is a class with students who have severe motivation problems and need intensified support and activating working methods instead of sitting in a chair and tanking up academic studies. They are proud of their new skills and want to become instructors for other students at the school.

Our STEAM Learning Environment is open every school day and serves the local community with the help of students when needed. It has opened a new world for many subject teachers, and the enthusiasm is tangible! The work done and great spirit have had positive effects to whole school community and other subjects. It has even broken the dams of the long-awaited need of co-operation between teachers. Also, many teachers have found motivation to learn new and elements for personal development through STEAM.

Due to this great success and good results, we have started co-operation with other schools that are willing to do the same.

STEAM is a way to do and enable cross-curriculum work. It is not meant to replace teachers' jobs or to function without human interaction. Neither is it meant to be implemented from one subject point of view only. We have to open the classroom doors and expand the concept of learning environment to let our students learn future skills together. I strongly recommend every school to try STEAM!

With STEAM, the students have more opportunities to train their skills and find their strengths.

2.5

REINFORCING STUDENTS' INVOLVEMENT AND PARTICIPATION

Kaisa Tuomarla (M.Ed.), Class teacher, Atala primary school (grades K-6), Tampere, Finland

Students' participation and involvement in school life, their own learning and the school culture in general is one of the cornerstones of the new Finnish curriculum:

> *"A learning community constructs its operating methods together. A school culture that promotes participation, realises human rights and operates democratically lays a foundation for the pupils' growth into active citizens. The pupils participate in the planning, development and evaluation of the activities in accordance with their developmental stage. They get experiences of being heard and appreciated as community members. The pupils' involvement in planning their own schoolwork and their group's activities is a natural way of reinforcing participation. The pupils play an important role in the planning of multidisciplinary learning modules. The pupils are also encouraged to become involved in planning and developing the activities of the school and the learning environment."* (Finnish National Agency of Education 2016.)

The education provider has the responsibility to promote students' participation. The school guarantees that the students have possibilities to take part in developing cooperation, planning the school and classroom rules, and taking part in evaluating and preparing the curriculum.

Why is students' active participation and involvement so important? If we consider the school as a mini society, a community, it requires the exact same things as the real-life society does. If we do not want to have passive citizens, why would we want to have passive students? Activating methods and participation enhance future skills: social skills, team-work abilities, tolerance and appreciation of diversity.

Learning is a social phenomenon: interacting with other people promotes learning. Students need to collaborate with others, solve problems together and interact. Having a possibility to interact, make peer reviews and have truly influencing their learning process develops students' intrinsic motivation.

How to do it: student unions

Student association activities offer an important channel for the participation of pupils. In Finland, students must have a union in every school, from primary school to high school. Every student is a member of the student union: the membership comes automatically, and it is free of charge. Each year, every class votes for their representative in the student union board. The board meets approximately every month and discusses the school's issues. There is always a teacher who is responsible for guiding the board. In lower secondary education and upper secondary education, the student unions work more independently, without a guiding teacher.

Student unions propose all kinds of school activities. They have an influence on the school's everyday life and have the possibility to organize events during the school year (examples of my school include a Valentine's Day event, and a reflector competition during dark mornings season). Student unions also raise funds in bigger events and use the funds for the benefit of all pupils of the school: they could, for example, buy footballs for every classroom and so on.

In lower and upper secondary schools, the students' unions have even more influence on school life and are directly involved in the school's decision-making.

If we do not want to have passive citizens, why would we want to have passive students?

How to promote participation: everyday choices in the classroom

Choosing methods

Finnish teachers have the freedom to choose the methods used in their classroom. The only regulatory factor is, in fact, the curriculum. Otherwise the methods and lessons are designed by a teacher. And when the teacher is free to choose the method, they can always engage the students, too, and let them decide.

All choices must be set in accordance with the students' developmental stage. The younger the children, the simpler choices there should be, such as choosing from two alternatives, or voting for the next lesson (the teacher can tell that the two next lessons are math and art, so which one comes first?). The experience of making decisions about lessons motivates the children.

Students as co-designers

Students can also co-design some lessons or choose their contents. The teacher's role is to define what kind of activities or skills students should practice. After that, students can think to themselves how they should do it. Here is a case example with physical education lessons: the topic of the lesson is handling a ball by throwing, catching and rolling it. Students in small groups can design the instructions, tasks and exercises. One of the groups can plan an exercise to practice throwing and catching, while another group can make up a game of it. The third group plans how to practice rolling and so on.

Learning contracts

Different kinds of learning contracts are a great way to get students involved. The teacher creates the topics for one day or even for a week, and the students choose (by themselves or with a friend or a group) in which order they will study these topics. The teacher is a guide who creates a self-help resource center: the center is a handout or poster, from which the students can learn about the topic themselves. The self-help resource center may contain guidelines, tips, hints and instructions for the topic being studied. The method is quite challenging for teachers, but it is absolutely worth it! This way children can learn about taking responsibility over their own learning. Of course, learning contract days and weeks require self-directedness and self-discipline, so it might be difficult for some children and students. Pairs and teams can be another helpful format for working on learning contracts.

Classroom incentives

Different kinds of class incentives are widely used to improve positive classroom behavior and performance. The class can set the goals they want to achieve. If the class is having trouble remembering to do their homework, the goal can be to reduce memory leaks for a few weeks. Other examples of common goals include not having quarrels during recesses, or everyone reading one book in two weeks. It is important to let the students choose the reward, too. The teacher can first collect all proposals for rewards, including the wildest ones ("Each kid gets their own yacht!"), and then use their right to veto: the teacher leaves only the feasible proposals for rewards, and the students vote for them.

All actions and decisions in which the students can participate strengthen their motivation and commitment to their own actions and deepen their learning.

Self-assessment

Students' self-assessment is integrated into the overall progress and achievement assessment and evaluation. Self-assessment is carried out every year and continuously throughout the school year during study periods. Mostly self-assessment is done on forms or blanks, but sometimes also in writings or in conversations in a group or with a teacher. The teacher can also run a quick round of students' self-assessment at the end of each lesson to reflect on what has been learnt and/or whether something needs to be reviewed.

Teachers use self-assessment as a base for the student's evaluation, assessment and parent-teacher-student conversations, which are held each year for every student. Self-assessment and reviews help students take responsibility and notice that they are responsible AND influential in their learning. Therefore, it is probably the most important way of participation.

As I have talked with the students during my years of teaching, they feel that self-assessment is valuable: "My opinion means something". I cannot imagine a better achievement of self-assessment and participation.

Reference

Finnish National Agency of Education 2016. *National core curriculum for basic education 2014.* Publications 2016:5. Helsinki.

3

EDUCATIONAL SUPPORT IN THE FINNISH WAY

Satu Herrala (MA), Special education teacher,
Takahuhti comprehensive school (grades 1–9) Tampere, Finland

Finland is a country where people believe in equal opportunities and education for all. Every pupil and student should have equal access to high-quality education and opportunities to maximize their potential and develop as learners. To be able to do so, the pupil may need educational support and guidance. In the Finnish school system, each pupil or student is entitled to educational support and pupil welfare services. Pasi Sahlberg (2015, 65) points out that "*Special education in Finland is for all students, based on the assumption that at some points of our lives all of us need support and help to move forward.*" As a result of this, almost half of Finnish 16-year-olds who have completed their basic education in comprehensive school have had some sort of special education or individual guidance during their time in school (Sahlberg 2015, 14).

The need of support is based on pedagogical observations

The use of supportive measures in Finland is never based on diagnoses, but on the actual needs of the pupil. The identification of the need for support

The use of supportive measures in Finland is never based on diagnoses, but on the actual needs of the pupil.

is usually based on the observations made by the class or subject teacher and special education teacher. Sometimes the initiative to start the support may come from the parents or the pupil. Psychological or medical assessments of the reasons for the learning or behavioral problems can provide valuable information on planning and executing the support, but the decision to start the support is pedagogical only. This ensures that valuable time is not wasted in waiting for the diagnosis. Sometimes the need for support at school can differ from that anticipated in medical statements.

> *It is good to remember that there is no need for medical diagnosis to receive support according to the basic education law. Comprehensive schools do not support pupils based on diagnosis but based on actual needs of the pupils. The school always works based on pedagogical solutions. This means that the school should provide all the needed support despite medical diagnosis.* (Sandberg 2017a.)

Educational support given to the pupil is always individually tailored, and changes can be made easily when the pupil's need for support changes. The use of supportive measures must be assessed regularly, and changes can only be made in co-operation with the pupil and the parents.

Co-operation is a key to pupils' learning and welfare

Although the decisions on educational support are made on a pedagogical basis, one cannot emphasize enough the need for close co-operation and communication with the homes. According to the National Core Curriculum (2016, 65), *"instruction and education shall be organized in co-operation with guardians"*. This co-operation becomes even more important when a child needs support.

Parents play an important role in supporting and encouraging their child's learning and school attendance. To be able to monitor each pupil's progress in studies and identify and meet the pupil's need for support, teachers need to co-operate with the pupil and the guardians. The parents must be informed of the possibilities of receiving support and the three-tiered system of support. The aim is always a good co-operation with the parents. However, a child's right to educational support is so strong that the parent cannot refuse to accept supportive measures at school. (National core curriculum for basic education 2016, 65.)

Efficient educational support is based on co-operation not only with the parents, but also with other professionals, such as the school psychologist, school social worker, school nurse or doctor. In addition to learning problems, the pupils may also have behavioral or emotional disorders. Teachers need shared expertise in form of multiprofessional co-operation to support the pupils, especially in challenges related to behavioral and emotional disorders. For this reason, the development of a collaborative school culture is emphasized in the Finnish education system (Lakkala et al. 2019, 127). Norvapalo and Thessler (2018, 10) find multiprofessional co-operation to be successful when it is clearly organized, people understand one another's job descriptions and recognize the capacities of different parties.

One school for all – inclusive education

The inclusion of children with special educational needs in mainstream schooling is an important guiding principle of Finnish education. The aim is to provide special needs education mainly in conjunction with mainstream education. The basic idea is that all pupils with learning difficulties are entitled to help and support to overcome these difficulties.

In the past, special education in Finland was segregating. There was a dual system of general and special education: one for pupils without any special challenges and one for those in need for support. Children with learning and other disabilities were taught according to a specific curriculum in special schools.

Nowadays, the goal of the educational policy is to strengthen inclusive structures in the school system in accordance with the international statements and agreements which Finland has signed and committed to (e.g. Salamanca statement, UNESCO, 1994). In 1996, Finland joined the European Agency for Special Needs and Inclusive Education, after which occurred a shift form the dual system towards more inclusive thinking. Lakkala et al. (2019, 126) point out that during the past two decades Finland has been developing a socially coherent system of more inclusive basic education by reforming The National core curriculum for basic education in 2010 and 2014. According to the new curriculum (National core curriculum for basic education, 2016, 19), basic education is developed in accordance with the principles of inclusive education. This tears down the boundaries between mainstream education and special education and makes educational support an integrated part of pedagogical practices in the schools (Ström & Hannus-Gullmets 2015, 6).

Earlier, pupils with special needs were picked up from their peer group and put to different kinds of special needs groups. Now, the idea is that in every class, there are many kinds of learners with different needs. Instead of moving children with special needs to separate special schools, every child should be provided with suitable supportive measures in their local mainstream schools. This requires co-operation between teachers, special education teachers, other professionals and homes. The aim is to ensure support and feeling of belonging for each pupil.

The number of special schools has been decreasing in most municipalities, and special classes have been moved into regular schools. It is the duty of the education provider (i.e. the municipality) to include pupils with special needs in the mainstream educational system. Thuneberg et al. (2013, 70) summarize the main principles of organizing the support:

> *... in the first place children should be taught in mainstream classes. The second-best choice would be flexible part-time small group setting and only then if even that does not meet the child's needs should a special class be considered.*

There are no different curricula for general and special education. Instead, all learners use the same curriculum individualized through Individual Education Plan (IEP).

Early intervention prevents further problems from arising

In Finland, special education needs are identified and addressed as early as possible. Early intervention means that problems at school are recognized and dealt with before they become more complex. It is important that support is given in the early stages of the child's development or as soon as the need for support becomes apparent. The sooner the child receives help, the easier it is to prevent the accumulation of problems. The identification of the need for support is based on observations made by the teacher, the parents and sometimes also other professionals (e.g. school psychologist). Supportive measures are then planned together with the pupil and their guardians.

The focus in early intervention is on child health care in child health clinics and early childhood education where learning and development problems can be identified before the child enters school. It is useful to start school with rather heavy supportive measures if there have been problems in early childhood education or pre-school. When the child gets a lot of support to start with, future problems might be avoided. Early intervention at school usually means that the child receives a lot of support in reading, writing and mathematics. Sahlberg (2015, 67) points out that as a result of this early support, the number of pupils in special education in Finland in the early years of primary school is relatively high compared to other countries.

Part-time special education is provided in all schools

In Finland, pupils get low-threshold support in their studies in form of the so-called part-time special education. It is given to pupils with minor learning or adjustment problems such as learning and writing difficulties, problems in mathematical or linguistic skills or difficulties in study skills. Special education teachers who give part-time special education are highly trained professionals with a university degree.

Part-time special education can be arranged simultaneously with regular class instruction, which means that a special education teacher attends regular classes to help certain pupils or the whole class together with the class or subject teacher. Part-time special education can also be provided as small group teaching (usually once or twice a week), or even individually. It does not mean that the pupils receiving part-time education would have a special education status, but instead they need short-term special education (Takala et al. 2008, 1). Getting part-time special education does not require any medical diagnoses or formal decisions, but receiving it is the right of every pupil if they have difficulties in their learning or school attendance. When a special education teacher co-teaches with a class or subject-teacher in a regular classroom, special education can be seen as an integral part of general classroom practices which benefits all pupils – not only those with special needs (Thuneberg et al. 2013, 71).

Finnish pupils have scored high in international student surveys and assessments such as PISA (Program for International Student Assessment) and TIMSS (Trends in International Mathematics and Science Study). Välijärvi et al. (2007, 48) state that one explanation to the success in academic studies has been the successful use of part-time special education. According to Kivirauma and Ruoho (2007), the PISA results reflect a high degree of equality and equity in the Finnish schools. They conclude (2007, 288) that it is reasonable to think that part-time special education has a key role in explaining the good results in PISA assessments. What is interesting in the results is that the gap between the top and low performers was smaller than in the other OECD countries. Especially the weakest pupils in Finland outperform the weakest pupils in other countries.

Three-tiered support model guarantees individual support

In 2010, new amendments regarding special education were made to the Finnish Basic Education Act (642/2010). The new three-tiered support system was introduced in 2011 along with the idea that all teachers – not only special education teachers – are responsible for evaluating planning and delivering support to their pupils. There are now three categories of support: (1) *general*, (2) *intensified* and (3) *special* support. The system is flexible, and pupils can move from one tier to another if the need for support changes.

The foundation of support is high-quality basic education for all. It is characterized by teachers' ability to plan and assess learning in the class and follow the development and progress of every child, their skills to guide and control the learning group, their communication and collaboration skills with other teachers, pupils and parents, and their ability to use different kinds of teaching and learning methods to create a comfortable learning environment and to organize multidisciplinary co-operation in order to support all the pupils. The key persons in the support system are class and subject teachers who notice the need for support and, in the first place, give the pupil support in co-operation with other teachers. In a way, in the Finnish system every teacher is a special education teacher. Thuneberg (2013, 71) points out that it is a true sign of professionalism when the teacher recognizes when it is time to seek consultation and help from special education teachers and student welfare team.

In every level of support, co-operation on regular basis is essential. Sandberg (2017a) points out that co-operation with the parents on a regular basis is very important, and the parents must be informed about the child's development and need for support along with the planned measures of support.

General support

The first response to a pupil's need for individual support is called general support. It is implemented for all pupils, and it is given as soon as the need

• • •

The key persons in the support system are class and subject teachers who notice the need for support.

• • •

arises. It can be provided to all pupils by a class teacher or a subject teacher. No evaluations, formal decisions or medical diagnoses are needed. General support is usually short-term support, and only one or two supportive measures are used at the same time. Part-time special education can be utilized in general support, but it is usually used in one or two subjects only and often for a short period of time. A learning plan can be written, but it is not mandatory. However, it is useful to write down the supportive measures the pupil has received.

A commonly used supportive measure in general support is remedial teaching which can be given by a class or subject teacher either during lessons or at other times. It is often given to pupils who have temporarily fallen behind in studies. It can be given even before any greater obstacles in learning appear. Remedial teaching and part-time education are support forms that are stipulated in the Basic Education Act (628/1998), and they can both be given at all levels of support.

In general support, the learning environment can be modified so that there are no distracting things in the classroom (Sandberg, 2017a). Teachers should also modify their teaching so that it meets the individual needs of the pupils. Modifying or differentiation of teaching and learning can involve materials and methods used, or the amount of classwork and homework or the time reserved for them. Sandberg points out that teaching everybody in the same way is not appropriate anymore. Finnish teachers are well-trained in differentiating and creating individual learning paths.

Sandberg (2017a) also describes other supportive measures commonly used in general support such as audiobooks and other technical tools, a well-structured school day, school assistant services and constant co-operation with the parents. The pupils also have the right to pupil welfare and guidance counseling services.

Intensified support

Sometimes the teacher may notice that general support is not enough to meet the needs of the pupil. The teacher then writes a *pedagogical assessment* which outlines the overall situation of the pupil. It consists of information on the supportive measures that have already been provided in general support, the pupil's strengths, interests and learning capabilities, a detailed analysis of their special needs as well as a suggestion for further support. This assessment can also include evaluations and test results from other experts, like the school psychologist. The parents are involved in the process, and their opinion is taken into account. The use of supportive measures is always based on recognizing the strengths of the students and building on them (Thuneberg 2013, 73). Sandberg (2017b) states that by concentrating only on the need of support based on disabilities, the teachers often forget that every pupil – even with massive learning problems – has many strengths that they can build on.

The assessment is then evaluated in the multiprofessional pedagogical team of the school which is responsible for the provision and monitoring of support. The pupil will now be moved to the second tier which is called intensified support. The measures on this tier are the same as in general support, but they are now more extensive and regular because of the student's need for long-term support. Usually the pupil needs more than one form of support. Part-time special education, individual guidance and co-operation with the parents are frequently used support forms in intensified support. (National core curriculum for basic education 2016, 66.)

Intensified support is given as a part of mainstream education, but the role of special education teacher becomes more intensive. The pupil will receive a lot of part-time special education from a special education teacher either in the classroom or in a smaller flexible group, sometimes even individually.

In intensified support, *a learning plan* is always drawn up for the pupil. The learning plan consists of the measures that are planned to support the pupil. They are concrete descriptions of organizing the learning environment, learning aids, forms of support and guidance and so on. According to the National Core Curriculum (2016, 68), the learning plan must always include the following information:

1. The pupil's views of their own goals and interests, strengths associated with learning, learning capabilities and special needs; the pupil's goals related to learning, working and school attendance
2. Pedagogical solutions (learning environments, support provided for the pupil, remedial teaching and part-time special education, measures of guidance counseling, possible priority areas of study in various subjects)
3. Co-operation and services required for support (e.g. pupil welfare and other experts, co-operation with the pupil and the guardian)
4. Monitoring and evaluation of the support

Sometimes it is useful to restrict the amount of learning content so that the pupil can use more time learning the basics and the most essential substance of the curriculum. In intensified support, it is possible to define the key content of the curriculum which then forms the target of learning. These are called *particular priority areas of study* (National core curriculum for basic education 2016, 73).

Intensified support can sometimes be organized as small group learning. Some schools have flexible part-time small groups where students can study for a part of their lessons for different periods of time and receive a lot of part-time special education from a special education teacher. One special form of small-group learning is *a class of flexible basic education* (in Finnish: "JOPO-class") which is intended for 8th and 9th graders who have motivational problems and benefit from activity-based learning methods and small-group learning with personal support and individual guidance.

Special support

If a pupil does not progress in learning and thus cannot achieve the goals of the curriculum even with the help of extensive intensified support, it is time to consider moving to the highest tier – special support. Special support is the most intensive form of support and requires an official decision. The purpose of special support is to provide the pupil with holistic and systematic help so that they can complete basic education and succeed in further studies after that. (National core curriculum for basic education 2016, 69.) In special support, all forms of support can be used, including full-time special education in a special class.

Before deciding on special support, an extensive *pedagogical statement* is made, where the situation of the pupil and the provided intensified support are described in detail by the teachers. Medical certificates and statements or test results from the school psychologist, for example, can be included in the statement, if needed (Sandberg, 2017a).

This information is then discussed multiprofessionally in the school welfare group, and a written account on the support is made. The education provider, often the principal of the school, makes an official decision to start the special support. The guardians and the student are heard during the process, and the decision is made in accordance with the Administrative Procedure Act. (National core curriculum for basic education 2016, 70.)

Special support includes broad and systematic supportive measures which are described in an individual education plan (IEP). In the IEP, learning is personalized to meet the learner's abilities. Sandberg (2017a) summarizes the IEP as follows:

> *The individual educational plan includes the special focus of teaching, the follow-up and evaluation of learning, different ways the pupil can show his/her know-how, the ways the pupil is evaluated, pupil's self-evaluation and other pedagogical solutions like flexible groupings, co-teaching, teaching methods, learning strategies, working methods, ways to communicate and learning materials.*

The IEP must be revised and updated every year in co-operation with the pupil and the parents. During the second and the sixth grades, the need for special support must be reviewed. If the pupil still needs special support, a new decision must be made. If the need for support changes or ends, a new decision is needed, too.

If a student needs special support in one or more school subjects, their learning objectives can be modified through the IEP. In this case, the objectives of the general curriculum are not applied, but instead are substituted by individual learning objectives and individual assessment defined in the IEP. According to the National core curriculum for basic education (2016, 73), this kind of individualization of the syllabus means that the achievement level for the pupil's learning is set to match the pupil's capabilities. The objectives and contents of the subject can be derived either from the syllabus of the same grade or from the lower grades, if needed.

Special classes and schools

Often, starting the special support means full-time need of special education, which is provided in a special class. In relation to the inclusive education dimensions, the special classes are usually located in mainstream schools instead of separate special schools, and special support can be given at the pupils' local school. This practice does not make Finnish schools totally inclusive, but it is a step towards more inclusive thinking as it will integrate pupils to their peer group during breaks and integrated lessons among others.

Every special class pupil must have a plan written down in their IEP about how and in which subjects they are integrated into mainstream classes. In most cases, the easiest way to integrate pupils is in the so-called non-academic subjects like music or arts. However, integration is always tailored individually, and if a pupil has good cognitive skills, they may be able to participate mainstream classes in other subjects, too.

There used to be separate special needs classes for different learning or behavioral problems. Nowadays, special classes are rarely formed based on diagnoses or the type of difficulties the children have. Pupils in local special classes may have very different types of problems ranging from learning problems to behavioral ones. Often, problems overlap, and one pupil may have several different difficulties. This means that the teacher meets many kinds of pedagogical challenges and needs broad special educational skills to solve them.

The municipalities and education providers may also have more specialized classes, as for pupils who need very demanding support for behavioral problems or have broad learning problems. These classes are usually smaller and have more teachers and school assistants.

For pupils who are unable to reach the goals of the subject-divided curriculum, in other words for pupils with very difficult developmental disabilities, there are special classes where learning and instruction are organized by so-called *activity areas*. They are functional life skills, like motor skills, social and cognitive skills, speech and communication and everyday life skills. The idea is to provide the pupils with skills that help them cope in their lives as independently as possible (National core curriculum for basic education 2016, 75). These classes are small, and there are many people working with these children who need a lot of help, support and medical care in their everyday lives.

There are still some state-owned special schools in Finland. Most of them belong to *Valteri*, the National Centre for Learning and Consulting that operates under the Finnish National Agency for Education. Valteri has six units in different parts of Finland where pupils in need for support can learn and receive rehabilitation. Valteri schools organize support periods for pupils and arrange consultation and training for parents and school staff. The idea is to support pupils' studies at their local schools in their own municipalities. (See valteri.fi/en/)

Finnish special education in statistics

After introducing the three-tier model of support in 2011, the number of pupils in intensified support has been growing steadily, reaching approximately 10% in 2018. The corresponding number in special support was 8%. This means that nearly one in five pupils in basic education has received intensified or special support. The statistics also show that the number of special schools has decreased during the recent years.

The share of pupils receiving all education in a special education group in a special school has fallen yearly and was only 8% of the pupils who received special support in 2018. The statistics do not contain information about general support as a whole, but they include data on part-time special education, which shows that 22% of pupils received part-time special education arranged as general support in 2018. (Official Statistics of Finland 2018.)

Welfare services are organized through multiprofessional teams

Pupils in basic education are entitled to pupil welfare services which are strongly linked with the three-tiered support system, thus being an important part of support on every tier. Pupil welfare provides care and support in the school's everyday routines. In the new support system, the focus on pupil welfare is strongly being moved from individual-centered problem-solving to early intervention and preventive measures (Thuneberg et al 2013, 74).

Pupil welfare services are organized by a multiprofessional team consisting of special education teachers, a school nurse, a social worker, a school counselor, a psychologist, a school doctor and the principal. Pupil welfare can be divided in *collaborative* and *individual pupil welfare*. The former includes preventive pupil welfare that supports the whole school community, such as co-operation between home and school and measures that promote well-being, safety, accessibility and good atmosphere. The participation of the pupils and guardians in these measures is important, and the education provider has the duty to promote the pupils' participation (National core curriculum for basic education 2016, 83).

Every pupil has the right to individual pupil welfare which "*aims to help the student learn, be healthy, experience well-being and a sense of inclusion, and help to prevent problems from arising*" (Ministry of Education and Culture, General Education, Pupil and Student welfare 2020). In practice, individual pupil welfare means school health services, services of a school psychologist, social worker and a multiprofessional group gathered for matters regarding individual pupils. Pupils receive these services free of charge. Individual pupil welfare in these expert groups is always based on the consent of the pupil and if necessary, the guardian (National core curriculum for basic education 2016, 84). The pedagogical team of the school, however, can deal with school-related problems of the pupil without any permissions, although co-operation with homes is always recommended. The pedagogical team usually consists of special education teachers, the class or form teacher of the student, the school counselor and the principals.

In conclusion

The Finnish system of supporting pupils at school has proven itself very effective. Especially part-time special education has been a key factor in explaining Finland's success in international surveys and assessments. Inclusive education emphasizes the right for every child to attend the nearest mainstream school. This has required changing the Finnish schools so that everyone can participate and learn together. The three-tiered support model ensures that no pupil is left behind, and everybody receives high-quality education and support. Special education teachers are a valuable resource in Finnish schools, and their expertise is needed when planning flexible arrangements that support every pupil. Co-operation between teachers, other experts, pupils and homes is the path to good results in the future, too. The focus must be kept in equity and well-being of pupils as well as in the joy of learning – in the Finnish way.

The three-tiered support model ensures that no pupil is left behind, and everybody receives high-quality education and support.

References

Kivirauma, J. & Ruoho, K. 2007. Excellence through Special Education? Lessons from the Finnish School Reform. *International Review of Education 53*:3, 283–302.

Lakkala, S., Takala, M., Miettunen, H., Kyrö-Ämmälä, O., Sarivaara, E., & Kielinen, M. 2019. *Steps towards and challenges of inclusive education in Northern Finland*. Collections, 196. University of Lapland. Accessed 12 March 2020. Retrieved from https://lauda.ulapland.fi/handle/10024/63723

Ministry of Education and Culture, General Education, Pupil and Student welfare Accessed 12 March 2020. Retrieved from https://minedu.fi/en/pupil-and-student-welfare

National core curriculum for basic education 2014 2016. Finnish National Board of Education. Publications 5. Helsinki.

Norvapalo, K. & Thessler, K. (Eds) *Multiagency in schools – Communal school welfare and support of transitions 2018*. University of Lapland.

Sahlberg, P. 2015. *Finnish Lessons 2.0. What can the world learn from educational change in Finland?* 2nd ed. New York: Teachers College Press.

Sandberg, Erja 2017a. *This is How We Do It: Supportive Measures in the Finnish Comprehensive School*. Accessed 12 March 2020. Retrieved from https://www.erjasandberg.eu/comprehensive-school/this-is-how-we-do-it-supportive-measures-in-the-finnish-comprehensive-school/

Sandberg, Erja 2017b. *Noticing strengths and focusing on what's positive makes a difference.* Accessed 12 March 2020. Retrieved from https://www.erjasandberg.eu/opetus/noticing-strengths-and-focusing-on-whats-positive-makes-a-difference/

Official Statistics of Finland (OSF) Special education 2018. *Nearly one in five comprehensive school pupils received intensified or special support.* 2018. Page on Statistics Finland website. Accessed 12 March 2020. Retrieved from https://www.tilastokeskus.fi/til/erop/2018/erop_2018_2019-06-19_tie_001_en.html

Ström, K. & Hannus-Gullmets, B. 2015. *From special (class) teacher to special educator: The Finnish case. Transitions in the field of special education.* Theoretical perspectives and implications for practice 115–134. Waxmann Verlag.

Takala, M., Pirttimaa, R. A., & Törmänen, M. 2009. Inclusive special education: the role of special education teachers in Finland. *British Journal of Special Education 36*(3), 162–172.

Thuneberg, H., Vainikainen, M., Ahtiainen, R., Lintuvuori, M., Salo, K., & Hautamäki, J. 2013. *Education is special for all – The Finnish support model.* Gemeinsam leben 2/2013. Beltz Juventa.

Välijärvi, J., Kupari, P., Linnakylä, P, Reinikainen, P., Sulkunen, S., & Törnroos, J. 2007. *The Finnish success in Pisa – and some reasons behind it: 2, PISA 2003.* Jyväskylä: Kirjapaino Oma. Accessed 12 March 2020. Retrieved from https://jyx.jyu.fi/bitstream/handle/123456789/37478/978-951-39-3038-7.pdf?sequence=1&isAllowed=y

3.1

GENERAL SUPPORT: THE FIRST RESPONSE TO A PUPIL'S NEED FOR INDIVIDUAL SUPPORT

Teemu Nieminen (M.Ed., M.Sc.), Teacher in basic education, Finland

Nearly all classrooms in Finland and abroad have over 20 students, and each of the students is an individual who learns in different ways. Some learners will remember everything by listening, while others must read and still others must write. Some students adapt knowledge best by using hands-on methods. That is what the Finnish student-centered learning is all about. Every student is entitled to equitable support for their learning.

General support is the first form of support for every student. General support responds to a student's individual needs. It is a natural part of everyday teaching and the learning process. This is generally referred to as differentiation, or individual pedagogical solutions, as well as guidance and early intervention support measures provided as part of the daily school life. The Finnish Ministry of Education and Culture also stresses that general support should be provided as soon as the need for support is detected, and without any special tests or decisions.

Because I am a class-teacher, I see my students every day during many lessons, and I know them and their strengths and weaknesses quite well.

• • •

General support should be provided as soon as the need for support is detected, and without any special tests or decisions.

• • •

In Finland, the same teacher also teaches the same class normally more than one year, which will allow for a more specific, deeper teacher-student relationship to form. This relationship could also form with subject teachers, but because of the limited exposure each week, it would take more time. Since I know my students, I can quite easily find the most convenient way to support them in their learning. Remedial teaching is one of the possible methods to provide general support for students, but I use many different kinds of general support during my lessons.

When teaching subjects which require a lot of reading and understanding, like history and science, I use specific groupings. Groups might include students who are very capable or who find reading very challenging. Sometimes these groups might have mixed students so students who need more support would have the possibility to enjoy the help of their peers. Sometimes the group can be formed based on the academic level of the students: the group might only comprise so-called "future scientists". When working in groups, I either use 'Jigsaws' or distribute content to the groups based on its level of difficulty. Expert groups can then teach the others, or we could have a gallery walk run by students with the purpose of learning from each other instead. Changing groups opens many doors and gives me the possibility to apply many different methods. In many cases, I can also put in more effort and time for students who really need my support.

Mathematics is an example of a subject that can be easy for someone and very hard for someone else. Thanks to good materials, like digital platforms and books, differentiation is easy to achieve in mathematics. When using books, I use my own code-language with my students, and they immediately know what the compulsory exercises for everyone are and what are the more challenging extra activities. On the other hand, when I use digital platforms, like Bingel by SanomaPro or Eduten, they will guide students by automatically differentiating exercises based on the level the students show in their work. Finally, the teacher can track all the work and answers a student has given to understand their individual challenges.

One of the cornerstones of the Finnish education is the way we do our assessment. We do not have any standardized tests during basic education. That gives me the possibility to take more care and give evidence-based support on the progress instead of grading 'perfection'. We do have a curriculum in Finland that gives us the learning objectives, but I still have the freedom to stress the content I consider the most important. I also have the possibility to use many different methods for the assessing of learning: I can use formative assessment, like different rubrics and projects to demonstrate learning. I could also use summative tests in a formative way, which means that I am using those more to give me feedback about my teaching or to give feedback to students about their learning.

Start general support by considering these strategies:

- grouping
- classroom seating management
- differentiation of the content
- teaching methods
- peer-teaching
- assessment
- books, games and materials
- remedial teaching

Albert Einstein wrote a long time ago that *"Everybody is a genius. But if we judge a fish by its ability to climb a tree, it will live its whole life believing that it is stupid"*. If we, as professional educators, will remember this, we will support every student the best possible way for that student.

3.2

FLEXIBLE BASIC EDUCATION – THE FINNISH WAY OF REGAINING THE LOST SCHOOL MOTIVATION

Satu Herrala (MA), Special education teacher, Takahuhti comprehensive school (grades 1-9) Tampere, Finland

Each year in April, I spend one week interviewing teenagers (and their guardians) who want to apply for a class of flexible basic education. Only 12 of them will be qualified, although every applicant would need and deserve to be admitted to the class. The students who would benefit the most from the Jopo year will be chosen. Who are these children and what is this class about? It is yet another success story of Finnish basic education, called Jopo® ('Jopo' being an acronym for words Flexible Basic Education in Finnish). The Jopo® program is intended for 9th graders (sometimes even for 7th and 8th graders) who lack motivation and run a high risk of exclusion from secondary education. These students are often underachievers who feel misplaced in the classroom and are not motivated by traditional teacher-led ways of learning. Instead, they benefit from learning by doing and small group learning with personal support and guidance.

For most of my students, Jopo® has been a way to regain the motivation and self-confidence needed for completing their basic education. Learning in a Jopo class is based on four cornerstones:

1. Small group learning which enables every student the support they need and the strong sense of belonging to a group
2. On-the-job learning which gives an opportunity to learn by working and work by learning
3. Different learning environments such as learning camps and field trips which strengthen the sense of belonging and give further opportunities to learn outside the classroom

4. Close co-operation with the guardians which makes the students feel that the adults in their lives are supporting them in their path towards completing basic education and moving on to secondary education schools

Jopo is not a special needs class, although our students often have many kinds of challenges both at school and home. The teachers are usually special education teachers who work together with youth workers or youth instructors in the Jopo class.

CEO for Foundation Youth and the founder of Studio Schools in the UK, Geoff Mulgan has said that teenagers learn best by doing things and they learn best by doing things for real, which in a way is the opposite of what mainstream education actually does. This is the very essence of Jopo. What we try to do is to get out of the classroom and go to the real world to do things for real. We use a lot of activity-based learning methods along with inquiry-based learning, co-operative learning and project learning.

The idea behind Jopo is that learning is a social phenomenon which occurs everywhere. The same idea of learning can be seen in the Finnish national core curriculum. In this sense, Jopo has been ahead of its time in its attempt to take learning out of the classroom and to connect the content of the curriculum into real-life contexts.

The most important ways to take learning to the real world are the on-the-job learning periods. We try to integrate work and learning so that students could learn by working and work by learning. In Jopo classes, learning work-life skills is essential. We pay attention to skills such as being at work on time, knowing the safety regulations or confidentiality policy of the company. The young learn how to apply for work, what to say in the job interview, how to introduce themselves and so on. These skills along with the more general life management skills, like cooperation, taking responsibility, solving problems, and making decisions, are part of the broad-based skills in the Finnish national core curriculum.

Studies on Jopo show that 90% of students improve their performance at school during the Jopo year.

Jopo activities are effective. Studies on Jopo show that Jopo has succeeded in reducing dropout rates, and 90% of students improve their performance at school during the Jopo year. They re-engage in school, begin to attend regularly, improve their grade point averages and complete basic education (Bonafield-Pierce 2018). That applies to my Jopo students, too. Each year, I feel so proud when I see how they make progress, regain their motivation and finally receive their school-leaving certificates.

Reference

Bonafield-Pierce, J. C. 2018. *From Passenger to Driver: Strengthening Self-Efficacy in Finland's JOPO Class Students*. Education Doctoral Dissertations in Leadership, 104. University of St. Thomas. Accessed 11 March 2020. Retrieved from https://ir.stthomas.edu/caps_ed_lead_docdiss/104

3.3

SPECIAL SUPPORT AND EDUCATION ARRANGED BY ACTIVITY AREAS

Johanna Kämäräinen (M.Ed.), Special education teacher, Rahola comprehensive school (grades 1-9), Tampere, Finland

Teaching in Finland is often arranged according to the subject-based curriculum. If a student struggles to achieve the objectives outlined in the curriculum, the curriculum's objectives, content, or methods can be individualized to better suit the student's skills.

If it is clear that the student is unable to cope with even the individualized curriculum, their instruction can be arranged by activity areas instead of the usual way of the division of subjects. The students of the activity areas class are often students who have severe disabilities, but the activity areas method can also be used with students with other kinds of disabilities or serious illnesses. The activity areas are distributed into motor skills, speech and communication skills, social skills, everyday life skills and cognitive skills (Finnish National Agency of Education 2016).

Our Rahola comprehensive school in Tampere (grades 1–6 and special education grades 1–9) is an ordinary Finnish basic education school where the national curriculum guides the studying. The majority of the students study in ordinary classes. However, the custom in Finland is to include all

• • •

The custom in Finland is to include all students together in same schools with students who have special needs.

• • •

students together in same schools with students who have special needs and to arrange teaching so that it meets everybody's needs. This applies to our school, too.

Our school has two classes where education is arranged by activity areas. The maximum number of students per class is six, and the class has both special needs teacher and special needs assistant. Our students' grade level ranges from preschoolers to 9th graders.

The starting point of the activity areas instruction is focusing on the student's strengths and interests. Each student has very distinctive needs, and the responsible parties for finding out the student's most important goals are the teacher along with other professionals and the family. When planning the goals, we already consider the future needs of the student and what individual needs they might have after 10 or 20 years from now. We strive for rehabilitating everyday life where the instructions of the therapists are realized as part of the school's daily life. The essential factors to consider include the transitions of students with physical disabilities (and using the correct hold and technique) as well as the students' individual needs and goals in terms of a functioning daily living.

Our day starts with a morning circle where we review the day's schedule. We use a lot of pictograms and signs to support the teaching. The activity areas classes go on a trip at least once each week. We think that inclusion in the community and learning life skills is of paramount importance. Skills such as traveling by bus, getting around the city and visiting the library or a café are important. Other great learning environments are the nearby forests and parks.

The instruction is constructed through adventures and experiences: music, handcrafts, visual arts and everyday life skills such as cleaning and baking are a central part of our teaching. Another important area is physical activity, especially various motoric movements, which are essential to rehabilitative school life. Our classes utilize various special activity programs such as Knill and Sherborne.

One can see many types of assistive devices in an activity areas class. In our class, one will find standing aids, wheelchairs, special needs seating, a dressing bench, a special needs toilet seat and an attachable rest for chairs. Some students also have their own aids for dining, such as their own mug or spoon. The students may also require pressure garment, corsets or other body supporting garments. The school staff uses these devices daily as per the therapists' instructions. Therapy (i.a. physical, speech or occupational therapy) is a significant part of the student's rehabilitation, so the visits from therapists also set the tone for our daily life.

Since our students often have difficulties with communicating, our classes use various ways of communicating. Many students have their own communicating book (AACi), and we practice using it every day. Today, smart devices are becoming ever more common, and applications for either supporting or replacing speech can be accessed on a tablet. One of our students has an eye gaze-enabled computer and a hand-controlled trackball for it. Some students utilize signs as additional support for communicating, while some may have motoric challenges, and the previously mentioned practices may be too challenging for them. If this is the case, the students can communicate via expressions, gestures or other assistive devices like the eye gaze-enabled computer. More often than not, the underlying issue behind defiant behavior is actually one related to difficulties in communicating, and so the student acts out as a response to not being understood. Everyday life is often significantly improved when a common way of communicating is found.

The most important thing is that individual habits and routines to work smoothly in everyday school life are found for each student. Every student is taken into account and included each day, and they are valuable as themselves. A functioning team (the teacher and assistants) is the foundation of everything, and information is shared actively in both directions. Team meetings are an essential part of a functioning everyday life.

One of the most rewarding things is to find a common way of communicating with a student after years of trying, or when a student surprises you by learning how to zip themselves without help. We are delighted to see any kinds of accomplishments! We do practice doing new things in our everyday school life, but we also focus on reinforcing already learned skills. The everyday school life of the activity areas class is rehabilitating and holistic, and a positive pedagogy along with warm interaction is one of the most important tools when working with special children and youngsters. The co-operation and support between home and school are irreplaceable and valuable assets for us, the educators.

Reference

Finnish National Agency of Education 2016. *National core curriculum for basic education 2014.* Publications 2016:5. Helsinki.

4

FINNISH PEDAGOGICAL LEADERSHIP

Elena Chukhlantseva (M.Ed.), ECEC Specialist, Learning Scoop, Tampere, Finland
Juha Lahtinen (MA), Partner, Learning Scoop, Tampere, Finland

Finnish schools are led and managed exceptionally well. It is the principals who lay the foundation for equality and trust in Finnish schools. The principals are in charge of ensuring that both the teachers and the students can perform at their best and achieve outstanding results. This article describes the Finnish way of defining pedagogical leadership and how it is enacted in everyday life.

Defining Pedagogical Leadership

The Finnish National core curriculum for basic education (2016, 15–16) states the values of basic education as follows: the uniqueness of each pupil and their right to a good education, humanity, general knowledge and ability, equality and democracy, cultural diversity as a richness, as well as the necessity of a sustainable way of living. These values determine the core task of Finnish education.

The core task constitutes the foundational block upon which the subsequent work, organizational operation and implementation of the core curriculum are built. It is therefore crucial for the pedagogy to shape the

• • •

It is crucial for the pedagogy to shape the leadership action, not the other way around.

• • •

leadership action, not the other way around. When pedagogy is integrated within leadership, leadership becomes an inclusive, facilitative practice of leading and guiding the process of teaching and learning in school.

The concept of pedagogical leadership incorporates multiple dimensions and layers. This obviously poses a challenge for formulating a neat and accurate definition. For instance, Taipale (2004, 72) summarizes that pedagogical leadership is "*the superior's ability to guide subordinates towards the common goal, make the specified visions and objectives visible and teach people to understand and interpret, as well as discuss and manage interaction by means of positive interdependence and openness.*"

Vella (2013, 132–137) discusses the concept of pedagogical leadership through the attributes of a good school leader who promotes values, motivates people and helps them develop, encourages teamwork, recognizes success, is consistent, learns to listen, steps out of the spotlight and plans for change. Thus, pedagogical leadership requires specific abilities and attitudes which are then reflected in the principal's actions and words, with the purpose of advancing the school's pedagogical activity.

Parrila and Fonsén (2016) define pedagogical leadership as follows:

1. Pedagogical leadership is guiding the personnel's learning, as well as the whole organization's culture, in such a way that the pedagogical perspective is the value basis for all decision making.
2. Pedagogical leadership is shared leadership: the responsibility for pedagogical quality and its development is shared with the whole personnel. Actions that make this possible are concrete leadership actions, or in other words, pedagogical leadership.

This perspective applies to both the individual and the organizational level. It brings leadership closer to people's interaction and networks as opposed to the centralized architecture, which is often present in the former hierarchical leadership styles. Pedagogical leadership is not assigned to a positional leader only. *Rather, it* becomes a function that can be shared.

If a Finnish principal would be asked what pedagogical leadership means to them, one might hear the following definition: "Pedagogical leadership is the principal's own theory of action formed from a pedagogical standpoint and implemented as day-to-day activity." That is an excellent thought! Pedagogical leadership as a theory of action is considered to shift transformational efforts from the realm of ideas into the world of action

(Schlechty 2009, 275). Pedagogical leadership crystallizes into the principal's own theory of action.

Schools as learning organizations

The discussion of the phenomenon of pedagogical leadership needs to be placed in a broader context of societal changes unfolding in Finland in the 1990s. It should also be considered from the perspective of the Curriculum reform of that time.

Alava, Halttunen and Risku (2012, 23) describe the contemporary school realities:

> *For the first time, principals were to take a genuine leading role in their own school's pedagogical practices, responsibilities and priorities, instead of just implementing legal regulations. ...[The] operating models no longer come from up high; instead, a principal needs to be capable of ensuring the viability of the school on their own and its ability to perform well in the long term. ...The road towards pedagogical leadership was paved.*

The structural shifts, increasing access to information and the need for a strengthened critical, problem-solving and innovative thinking brought about new challenges and opportunities. The schools could no longer afford to be driven by compliance and control. Bureaucracies designed to regulate and manage organizations, people, responsibilities and tasks in a routine and accustomed fashion have been gradually displaced by a new type of organization – that of the learning organization.

Schlechty (2009, 50) states that in learning organizations, power and authority follow knowledge. The transition towards learning organizations in the 21st century implied that schools needed to strengthen their status as platforms for learning instead of platforms for instruction.

Solely reforming teaching and learning would be insufficient for the education system, which needed to respond to the realities. The concept of pedagogy would need an update in the 21st century, too, as Male & Palaiologou (2015, 216–221) comprehensively review. Pedagogy should go beyond the traditional context of subject teaching and learning. It should no longer occur in isolation or exclusively in the classroom. Instead, pedagogy should become an approach that looks after the ecology of the entire education community. Pedagogy is now the creation and cultivation of the learning environment which enables interactions and relationships between various stakeholders, or learners, in order to jointly construct knowledge.

Ultimately, these views and developments have changed the school principal's work in Finland. The need for increased engagement, learning community, capacity building and leadership practices – all aligned along the pedagogical continuum – have become essential. Pedagogical leadership must then be viewed as a network of development processes, as a work in progress, where learning is cultivated (Alava, Halttunen & Risku 2012, 36; Male & Palaiologou 2015, 220–229).

Systems thinking as a framework for pedagogical leadership

Education is a social institution, and the school is a mechanism for its realization. The way a school operates is a combined effort of many players who give a sense of meaning and continuity to the enterprise of learning. Pedagogical leadership as a type of leadership in the school is the holistic leadership of people, things and knowledge that utilizes people's collectiveness, differences, and innovativeness (Amke 2012, 5). It is, therefore, characteristic of pedagogical leadership to encompass many tangible and intangible parts.

Pedagogical leadership in the learning organization can be viewed through the lens of systems thinking. Systems thinking helps to gain insight into how leadership functions and evolves when pedagogical thinking permeates the entire school operation. It is a tool which the school's leader can use to create and maintain systematic and purposeful operation in their school.

The systems can be described in terms of elements, interconnectedness and purpose – all of which are equally important (Meadow 2008, 11–17). The underlying notion is that the elements, interconnectedness and purpose of a school's operation are parts of pedagogical leadership if they satisfy the school's primary core task – learning and the promotion of learning.

The elements of the school system are usually both fixed and temporary elements. They are accumulated over time and often can be easily measured. These elements provide the framework for actions and practices. Examples of the elements include the infrastructure, classrooms, supplies, materials, teachers, learners, administrators among others. Interconnections in the school system are relationships, interactions, feedback and flows of resources that hold the elements together. Interconnections are dynamic. These are, for instance, budgets, standards, qualifications, work schedules, teaching methods, leader's strategy, knowledge creation, incentives and so on. The purpose of the system is defined through what is happening in the school on every-day base. The purpose does not always derive from the educational policy documents by default, but it is what is observed through the system's behaviors and action.

The school system is nested within other systems, while it simultaneously has sub-systems that all are defined through their own unique elements, interconnections and purposes. For instance, the budget cuts and the changes in the structure of the education sector governance in the 1990s accelerated the development of practical management and strategic management as central parts of the work of a Finnish principal.

Moreover, when one or more elements, interconnections and purposes change, the system and therefore the pedagogical leadership will be continuously re-shaped in some way. To provide an example, a change in the assessment practices of schools would alter both the teaching methods as well as the students' learning experiences and well-being.

From the systems thinking perspective, the task of pedagogical leadership is not to only recognize the interplay between elements, interconnections, and purpose in the system but also to work towards unifying and optimizing all of the parts together. Therefore, pedagogical leadership amounts to more than leading the sum of the parts; it also looks beyond the structures and roles into the linkages and processes that deliver value to the entire organization.

The systems thinking approach implies that the school's functioning is neither a linear nor a fully rationalized process. It also promotes a different view of learning in which learning is ubiquitous, persistent, and flexible. The need to learn, experiment and interact is what strengthens the development of the system capacity to be adaptable in the uncertain future. When the system understands its nature, dynamics, potential and constraints, it can lead the complexity better.

The many roles of a school leader

There are several domains of action that the school leadership needs to embrace. The National Board of Education (2013, 14–15) defines the domains as follows:

1. Pedagogical work (the organizing of teaching, curriculum work, preparation and implementation of annual work planning and evaluation), school's development work and related individual and the whole school competences, management of learning, pedagogical networking (co-operation with educational institutions), pupil/student welfare, compliance with the terms of a collective agreement;

2. Human resource management (personnel allocation, substitutes, training, distribution of labor, distribution of lesson hours, well-being at work, developmental discussions);
3. Financial management (budget planning and monitoring, investment plans, billing);
4. General administrative tasks (statutory tasks and cooperation with various official bodies, statistics, reporting);
5. Development work, strategic planning, communication and various types of evaluation work;
6. School's own independent projects, external projects and the organization of personnel training, multi-professional cooperation.

According to many doctoral theses analyzed by Alava, Halttunen and Risku (2012), the operating field of schools, principals and teachers is becoming more and more complex and challenging. At the same time, a large number of schools have merged their operation. This means that an individual principal may supervise several school sites, despite the fact that the sites can be situated far away from each other. Depending on the availability of resources and distribution of powers in different municipalities, the principal's duties may cover an even broader range of responsibilities (for example, that of the head of education department, director of municipal educational and cultural services etc.).

The managing of resources that are characteristic to the school system requires the school leader to have an extensive set of leadership skills and competences. Therefore, in Finland, one must be a teacher first in order to become a school principal. The professional requirements for the principal's position are a Master's degree in class teaching or subject teaching, work experience as a teacher and a qualification in school leadership, management and administration. In addition, the principal of a Finnish school is the representative of the employer, usually a city or a municipality.

Pokka (2017, 72–77) observes that for decades, the strength of Finnish education politics has been the fact that the professional skills of principals are utilized in both national and local education planning. Each principal has the opportunity to take part in the discussion around education politics through various reference groups. At the same time, the principal communicates with the teachers, students and families. The two-way communication provides the school leaders with the opportunity to steer and influence educational matters and put their school-specific set of knowledge, expertise and competences to use.

However, the most vital part of a principal's work is to lead the school pedagogically (Pokka 2015, 55). All types of action (with the objectives of quality teaching and the well-being of the community) taking place in a school are considered to be a part of pedagogical leadership. In this sense, pedagogical leadership is seen as daily activity. When executed systematically, it promotes learning, improves learning performance and generates fulfillment throughout the organization.

Pedagogical leadership is leading for learning. It is a network of development processes. Pedagogical leadership is the key to ensuring that the organization's development processes form an integrated whole. In order for the school to be able to respond to the ever-changing realities, it is essential that pedagogical leadership strengthens and develops the school's capacity to adjust and innovate on a continuous basis.

It is important to purposefully and consistently explore what the existing system has to offer and what the future aspirations are. Furthermore, it is necessary to understand that development processes need to be led. It is precisely the leadership required by development processes that makes them key practical pedagogical leadership tools and channels of influence for a principal (Alava, Halttunen & Risku 2012, 38).

Pedagogical leadership is always future-oriented. The leader's role is to show the direction. A clearly articulated vision and need for change are the prerequisites for having the school onboard. The leader must also ensure that the school understands what resources are required for taking action, or what kinds of changes are necessary to support developments and innovations. From time to time, the underlying beliefs and ideas need to be critically examined. It is necessary to ponder whether the school's current situation meets the demands of time, whether the available solutions are in line with the laws and policy documents that guide the action and whether the practices are consistent with new educational knowledge (Fonsén 2019, 11).

The development of a clear vision is closely linked to the National Core Curriculum, which is the most important management tool of a school. It is a strategic and pedagogical tool that defines the policies for the education

Pedagogical leadership is the key to ensuring that the organization's development processes form an integrated whole.

provider's operation and the work carried by schools. Pokka (2017, 72) describes that other educational objectives are set in the local curriculum on the basis of the national curriculum, the national distribution of lesson hours, laws; in national and local development plans for education and research; and finally, in the strategic plan of the education provider. These objectives are actualized in the school's annual operating plan.

The local curriculum is an important part of the steering of education on-site. It plays a key role in setting out and implementing both national targets and tasks that are considered important locally. The local curriculum lays a common foundation for daily schoolwork in addition to setting its direction. The curriculum links the operation of the school to other local activities with the aim to promote students' well-being and learning. (National core curriculum for basic education 2016, 9). The local curriculum is the result of shared co-creation and collaborative work of the school community. As a consequence, curriculum design requires broad interaction that involves the teachers and principals working together, trusting each other and taking shared responsibilities.

In addition, every school must establish its own basic mission; the mission gives both meaning and justification to the school's existence and operations, as Alava, Halttunen and Risku (2012, 40) state. Every school realizes their own mission by implementing the curriculum along with the school's own perspectives or points of focus. Schools located in cities or in municipalities may differ in their missions, but they are always consistent with the beliefs and standards described in the local curriculum. The curriculum and the school's mission determine the present and the future action that the leader brings for a pedagogical discussion within the school.

The curriculum is a living and evolving tool. Its implementation must be always carried out with the future in mind – it is not enough for the school to be well-functioning today. Pedagogical leadership needs to be based on strategic thinking and action. Strategic action commits to the fact that any learning, change or innovation in the school needs enough time to ensure the intended action will be realized rather than remain a fragmented initiative without a consistent impact. Strategic leadership is also expressed in the leader's activity of developing the work community and leading people. This requires the school leader to create a system of support for the school's work community in order to enable its members to successfully fulfill their educational tasks.

The leader's important type of support relates to the pedagogy in the school. The management of pedagogy gives the direction to teaching and learning. The objectives are the development of teaching and education, the promotion of learning as well as the organization of quality education and teaching. The leader is responsible for the overall pedagogical standard of the entire school. Planning, implementation, evaluation and development of educational activities are basic processes in the management of pedagogy. The pedagogical approach also concerns the development of learning environments and learning methods that are student-centered and promote learning.

In Finland, the school leader stays in touch with everyday pedagogy by being visible and available for the school personnel. One of the reasons as to why the leader knows the everyday work of teachers first-hand is because they are also an expert in pedagogy, thanks to their background in professional training and work experience. A leader who is familiar with the practices by having inside information is capable of providing professional support to the teachers and to guide the development of their pedagogical self-leadership.

Competent and qualified personnel form one of the key resources of the educational organization and thus contribute to the school's capacity building. The personnel's competences are the cornerstones of quality education provision and the overall well-being of the school. They are an asset of the organization on the condition that continuous learning of the personnel is promoted. Learning, however, starts with the leader. The leader should assume the role of a learning leader rather than that of an expert leader. The reason for this is that the learning leader aims to foster the view that things can be learned and, ultimately, they can be applied in practice. The school principal's professional development and performance is reviewed annually.

Examining the teaching personnel's competencies, development needs and knowledge management is necessary (Alava, Halttunen & Risku 2012, 38). Annual individual professional development discussions and performance reviews are normal practices in Finnish schools. The leader sees the teacher as the owner of their professional development. A teacher's motivation and well-being are essential factors in the continuous knowledge development and should therefore be taken into account. From this perspective, pedagogical leadership is particularly emphasized in human resource management.

Instead of constantly holding teachers accountable for their activities and performance, the principal trusts them. Nevertheless, trust in the teacher, who enjoys great pedagogical freedom and professional autonomy in Finland, does not come alone: trust always goes hand in hand with responsibility, collaboration, and equality in the work community. Trust is the bond that holds wide-ranging knowledge and expertise together in the school. Trust is also based on the type of thinking that aims to find a process-like way to develop the core operations instead of looking for mistakes or acts of negligence (Pokka 2017, 142). Therefore, the school leader is never an inspector in any sense; rather, they perform in a manner that resembles a mentor or a coach who supports the teachers by showing them their potential and by supporting them in what they need in order to thrive and grow. The principal must have a strong expertise in adult learning.

Pedagogical support is also provided to the personnel in the form of in-service training. The professional training aims to correspond to the development goals that are identified during the teacher's professional development review, are brought by the changes in educational objectives or are defined by anticipated future needs. There are usually two types of trainings available: obligatory short-term trainings on common themes for all teachers and optional trainings on interest-specific themes. The professional trainings are organized by various local, regional, and national educational providers in face-to-face, online or blended formats. However, the general understanding has been that the fragmented and short-term nature of the in-service training does not necessarily allow for neither developing sufficient knowledge nor supporting the impact of what is newly learned. As maintained by Pokka (2017, 139–140), the transition towards planning longer and more multidimensional in-service training courses has already begun.

A leader committed to the creation of a functional and effective organizational culture highlights a leadership approach based on the interaction and collaboration between all the people inside the school community. Many of the principals' theories of action identified interaction between different actors as the characteristic of a good school (Hellström 2006, 37). The leader's task is to develop various ways of promoting the personnel's participation and committed decision-making in the school (National Board of Education 2013, 16, 26). The teachers' involvement in planning, operations and development work is a part of the entire organization's expertise development. When social boundaries are permeable, there is room for constructive action to take place (e.g. co-teaching, multidisciplinary study units, early intervention and welfare support to a student). In addition, opening the school to the environment around it has increased a principal's need to network (Jouttimäki 2006, 60).

Shared pedagogical leadership

Despite the fact that the supervisory role at comprehensive schools and general upper secondary schools has been centralized to the principal, performing all leadership functions by one single person is considered challenging and even unnecessary in the context of a learning organization. The division and decentralization of tasks between various school community members within the school is seen as a possible solution to this problem (National Board of Education 2019, 236). Thus, pedagogical leadership becomes an inclusive practice. Managing pedagogical activity is the school's core process and it involves the whole school's working community.

As Taipale (2012, 11–13) states, Finnish principals are relatively independent forces in their own school. There is no official hierarchy among the principals and the teaching profession in Finnish schools. Due to these facts, the design of the leadership structure depends on the discretion of the school community itself while there is no legal basis for it. Job descriptions and the distribution of powers are then recorded in the standing orders of procedure, which is approved by the school. The public sector's collective agreement system steers the solutions to some extent, if needed.

Shared leadership has been widely advocated as a model that offers the solution to successfully managing many of the school leadership roles and realizing the broad pedagogical leadership (National Board of Education 2013, 16, 27–28). Shared leadership refers to the involvement of the whole work community in the joint preparation of school activities, joint planning, joint decision-making process and joint responsibilities for action. The school members need to share the values, visions, objectives, ambitions, practices, strategies and frameworks in order to promote and support students' learning process. Shared leadership creates the sense of inclusion and ownership and, through them, the sense of community. Shared leadership makes it possible to exploit the full potential of the organization. However, sharing authority does not mean to give up authority.

Pokka (2017, 53) implies that in order to better suit the needs of school leadership and management, it is crucial to build a genuine shared leadership structure. The Finnish shared pedagogical leadership model can be said to

Shared leadership creates the sense of inclusion and ownership and, through them, the sense of community.

provide the optimal allocation of resources with minimum perplexity. Shared leadership implies clear structures and roles, and it comprises two elements – leadership activity and team organization activity.

The actual management structure of a Finnish school is rather flat. The school principal has an overall responsibility for the management process, and they must ensure that the process is open, and decision-making is transparent. Usually, schools have a principal and a vice principal, as well as one or more assistant principals as the school size increases.

With the reference to the Finnish and international research, Ahtiainen et al. (2019, 250) state that the delegation of single tasks is considered to be only the first steps in the development of the functional, shared pedagogical leadership. Shared pedagogical leadership is actualized not only in formally agreed roles and responsibilities but rather in the relationships and interaction between various members of the school's work community. Such interactions are enabled and facilitated in teams. Working in a team is a format that allows for necessary dialog and dynamics in the process-oriented, shared pedagogical leadership, where every member of the organization is a learner. Each school functions on a particular team structure.

Taipale (2006, 130–138) identifies three types of professional teams within the school community: leadership teams, development teams and learning teams. Leadership teams are formed to support the principal in leading the school towards a collectively developed vision of the future. Development teams usually have long-term development tasks that are often connected to the whole school's development, such as curriculum development work or an internal audit of the school's performance. Learning teams' tasks are aligned with the teachers' basic tasks of teaching and guiding learning. Typically, the learning teams are groups of teachers of the same grade level or of the same subject or field of study as well as multidisciplinary groups.

Shared pedagogical leadership is seen as daily activity in Finnish schools. It is also for this reason that the school's professionals are able to engage in persistent and continuous know-how sharing, peer exchange, collegial support and everyday decision-making, along with innovative and creative thinking and action.

In sum, shared leadership is about synergy in action, where the whole is greater than the sum of its parts (Amke 2012, 18). If leadership is not a shared function in the school, the agreements upon school processes and their implementation are not likely to become collective practices aimed to work in the same direction and towards the same goals.

Depending on the size of the school or the number of schools the principal supervises, the shared pedagogical leadership structure may be complemented by other approaches to leadership within the school (e.g. distributed leadership, sustainable leadership). Various leadership approaches are not necessarily mutually exclusive, rather they address different dimensions of the leadership structure. Fonsén et al (2015, 120) underlines that the leadership structure needs to be designed in such a way that it is complementary, where agents complement each other's knowledge and expertise while they also balance each other's lack of knowledge and expertise.

References

Ahtiainen, R., Lahtero, T. & Lång, N. 2019. Johtaminen perusopetuksessa — Katsaus koulujen johtamisjärjestelmiin ja rehtoreiden näkemyksiin johtajuuden jakamisesta [Leadership in basic education — A review of school management systems and principals' views on shared leadership]. In J. Hautamäki, J., Rämä, I., & Vainikainen M-P. (toim.) *Perusopetus, tasa-arvo ja oppimaan oppiminen* [Basic education, equality and learning to learn]. Helsinki: Yliopistopaino Unigrafia.

Alava, J., Halttunen, L., & Risku, M. 2012. *Changing school management*. Publications 2012:13. Edita: Prima.

Amke. 2012. *Kartta pedagogisen toiminnan johtamiseen* [A map for leading pedagogical action]. Accessed 03 March 2020. Retrieved from https://www.amke.fi/media/julkaisuja/kartta-pedagogisen-toiminnan-johtamiseen.pdf

Fonsén, E., Akselin, M-L., & Aronen, K. 2015. From distributed leadership towards joint leadership – a case study: the early stages of developing a new ECE leadership model for the City of Hämeenlinna. In Waniganayake, M., Rodd, J., & Gibbs, L. (Eds.). *Thinking and Learning about Leadership: Early childhood research from Australia, Finland and Norway*. Research Monograph #2. Sydney: Community Child Care Cooperative NSW. Accessed 03 March 2020. Retrieved from http://ilrfec.org/wp-content/uploads/2017/09/thinking-about-leadership-2015-09.pdf

Fonsén, E., 2019. Johda pedagogiikkaa [Lead the pedagogy]. Varhaiskasvatuksen Opettajien Liitto [Early Childhood Education Teacher's Union of Finland]. Helsinki: Print Line.

Hellström, M. 2006. Johtamisen haltuunotto omaa käyttöteoriaa konstruoimalla [Taking control of management through construction of one's own theory of action]. In Taipale, A., Salonen, M., & Karvonen, K. (Eds.) *Kuorma kasvaa – voiko johtajuutta jakaa? Kokemuksia oppilaitosjohtamisen hyvistä käytännöistä* [The growing load – can leadership be shared? Experiences of good practices in school management]. Opetushallitus. Helsinki: Hakapaino.

Jouttimäki, R. 2006. Oppilaitosjohtaminen on erilaisuuden johtamista [School management is the management of diversity]. In Taipale, A., Salonen, M., & Karvonen, K. (Eds.) *Kuorma kasvaa – voiko johtajuutta jakaa? Kokemuksia oppilaitosjohtamisen hyvistä käytännöistä* [The growing load – can leadership be shared? Experiences of good practices in school management]. Helsinki: Opetushallitus.

Lahtero, T. et al. 2019. Finnish principals: Leadership training and views on distributed leadership. *Educational Research and Reviews 14*(10), 340–348.

Male, T., & Palaiologou, I. 2015. Pedagogical Leadership in the 21st century: Evidence from the field. *Educational Management Administration & Leadership 43*(2), 214–231.

Mattila, P., & Silander, P. 2015. *How to create the school of the future.* Oulu: Multiprint. Accessed 03 March 2020. Retrieved from http://www.finpeda.fi/wp-content/uploads/2019/02/How-to-Create-the-School-of-the-Future_book.pdf

Meadow, D. 2008. *Thinking in systems: A primer.* US: Chelsea Green.

National Board of Education. 2013. *Rehtorien työnkuvan ja koulutuksen määrittämistä sekä kelpoisuusvaatimusten uudistamista valmistelevan työryhmän raportti* [The report of the working group on the reform of principals' job description, education requirements and eligibility criteria]. Raportit ja selvitykset [Reports and reviews]. 2013: 16. Helsinki: National Board of Education.

National Core Curriculum for Basic Education 2014. 2016. Finnish National Board of Education. Publications 5. Helsinki.

Parrila, S., & Fonsén, E. (Eds.). 2016. *Varhaiskasvatuksen pedagoginen johtajuus. Käsikirja käytännön työhön* [Pedagogical leadership in early childhood education. A guide to working practices]. Jyväskylä: PS-kustannus.

Pokka, A. 2017. *Top class: The Finnish school leadership and management.* Cultural Coop Vehrä & Bookcover.

Schlechty, C. P. 2009. *Leading for Learning: How to transform schools into learning organizations.* San Francisco, CA, US: Jossey-Bass.

Taipale, A., Salonen, M., & Karvonen, K. (Eds.) 2006. *Kuorma kasvaa – voiko johtajuutta jakaa? Kokemuksia oppilaitosjohtamisen hyvistä käytännöistä* [The growing load – can leadership be shared? Experiences of good practices in school management]. Opetushallitus. Helsinki: Hakapaino.

Taipale, A. 2012. *International survey on educational leadership. A survey on school leader's work and continuing education.* Finnish National Board of Education. Accessed 03 March 2020. Retrieved from https://www.slideshare.net/ghalebkandeel/143319-international-surveyoneducationalleadership

Taipale, M. 2004. *Työnjohtajasta tiimivalmentajaksi. Tapaustutkimus esimiehistä tiimien ohjaajina ja pedagogisina johtajina prosessiorganisaatiossa.* [From supervisor to team coach. Case study of leaders as team tutors and pedagogical leaders in a process organization]. Acta Universitatis Tamperensis 1033.

Vella, K. 2013. Working with People and for People. In Bezzina, C., & Vella, K. (Eds.) *The Leadership Imperative – A journey where people matter.* Malta: Print it.

4.1

WHAT ARE GOOD PRINCIPALS MADE OF?

Riitta Juusenaho (PhD, Ed.), Trainer, TOP School Consulting, Kangasala, Finland

The qualities of a good leader are difficult to define. The same cannot be stated about poor leadership, which is characterized by Finnish academic Paavo Haavikko (1931–2008) as everything being "always equally important in an ever-changing order".

As the school organization's traditional hierarchies are dismantled and we move towards shared leadership and team organizations, the principal's role as the school's pedagogical leader is emphasized. Teacher education alone is not enough for the challenging position of the principal, which requires not only understanding the curriculum's content, goals, and strategies, but also the national and local societal aspirations, finances and resource allocation, school culture, educational legislation and regulations, pedagogical and didactic methods, assessment guidelines, interacting with all stakeholders, personnel policy, property management, school transportation and psychosocial needs. This list could very well be endless. As I see it, there is an existing demand for a principal's own profession and a specific principals' education program for universities, such as the one offered by the University of Jyväskylä in Finland.

Finnish legislation defines the required qualifications of principals in addition to teacher training. In Finnish context, the term "principal" is commonly used instead of "headmaster". This is another way of differentiating between the school management profession and the teaching profession.

The principal represents the school

The most demanding and significant task of the above-mentioned list is, in my opinion, the principal's ability and competence as a human resource manager. A skilled principal succeeds in surrounding themselves with a competent, versatile staff which shares common goals and vision. The principal accepts the idea of shared leadership and sees its benefits while being ready to relinquish their exclusive authority. In a similar manner, they develop the work community towards a team organization so that the unified expertise of all the teachers can be leveraged to daily serve the school's productive and impactful activities.

It is important for the principal to lead their unit from the front, not from the behind or the middle. I consider it important to clearly distinguish the principal's profession from that of the teacher's, as well as that leadership training lays emphasis on the demanding, often lonely, role of the principal's profession. The principal is not only "one of the teachers", since they are the employer's representative at the school and must, therefore, act accordingly. The principal must keep in mind the equality and equity of both pupils, their families and the personnel. Additionally, a life-long learning attitude is a prerequisite for good school management.

Social capital guarantees well-being and productivity at work

The concept of social capital is considered complex. The formal dimension of the social capital entails the social networks that people create and the ways in which these networks are organized (cf. the teachers' lounge). In addition to that, social capital is strongly associated with trust, which is another dimension of the same concept.

Networks remain solid if their members feel the trust, adhere to common rules, share the same values and meet each other's expectations (cf. school spirit). Mutual trust builds capital for the community and its members for them to use. As defined by the OECD (2001), social capital grows and increases

● ● ●

A skilled principal succeeds in surrounding themselves with a competent, versatile staff which shares common goals and vision.

● ● ●

only when it is used. It cannot be stored for bad times as it disappears if nobody uses it (e.g. Coleman 1988). A skilled principal promotes the social capital of their work community.

Shared leadership, teamwork, shared values and respect for individuals, a solution orientation and a leadership allowing for failures guarantee the success of the principal's work. The more social capital the work community has, the healthier the members of it feel. Well-being at work guarantees the best results and quality in the organization.

A skilled principal creates personnel-oriented working methods in the work community and listens and accepts the opinions differing from their own. They share responsibility and authority equally while retaining the ultimate responsibility of leadership. They create stability in volatile situations, support personnel in conflicts and makes themselves visible in the school corridors. A skilled principal is easy to approach, humane, and well-balanced.

A skilled principal trusts their subordinates. They do not need to have their finger in every pie; they encourage the personnel to make independent decisions. A skilled principal is also an expert in emotional leadership, which helps them in getting the personnel's feelings support the school's goals (e.g. Sergiovanni 1991).

Another attribute of a skilled principal is that they take care of their own physical and mental health. The loneliness experienced by principals, which has been researched in many studies, is facilitated when principals form their own teams and share their feelings, and thus create social capital for their own leadership.

In their study, American scholars Schmieder, McGrevin and Townley (1994, 285) look for the critical skills of principals in order to find the key functions with which a new principal can successfully lead their school. According to the study, the principal should be aware of themselves and the direction in which they wish to develop their school. In other words, they must have a vision. Another emphasized aspect in this study was the principal's social skills.

It is clear that no matter how skilled the principal, they will not be very successful in their job if they are alone. The work community's support for the principal's work is essential. Similarly, finding a reference group and partnering with other principals supports peer learning and coping at work.

References

Coleman, J. 1988. Social Capital in the Creation of Human Capital. *The American Journal of Sociology 94.* Supplement: Organizations and Institutions: Sociological and Economic Approaches to the Analysis of Social Structure, 95–120.

OECD. 2001. *The Well-Being of Nations. The Role of Human and Social Capital.* Paris: Author.

Schmieder, H., McGrevin, C. Z., & Townley, A. J. 1994. Keys to success: Critical Skills for Novice Principals. *Journal of School Leadership, 4*, 273–293. CA: Technomic Publishing Co.

Sergiovanni, T. J. 1991. *The Principalship. A reflective practice perspective*. Boston: Allyn & Bacon.

4.2

DEVELOPING POSITIVE, CONSTRUCTIVE OPERATIONAL CULTURE AT SCHOOL

Tommi Roininen (M.Sc.), Assistant principal, Hakkari lower secondary school (grades 7–9), Lempäälä, Finland

"Culture is defined as the learned beliefs, values, rules, norms, symbols, and traditions that a group of people shares. The group that shares these qualities makes them unique." (Northouse 2007, 302)

According to the national core curriculum in Finland, the school culture plays a key role in implementing comprehensive basic education and thus always affects the quality of schoolwork experienced by the pupils (Finnish National Agency for Education 2016, 27).

The operational culture is an entity which consists of several components:

- interpretation of the norms that direct the work and the goals of activities
- leadership and the organization, planning, implementation and evaluation of work
- competence and development of the community
- pedagogy and professionalism
- interaction, atmosphere, everyday practices and learning environments. (Finnish National Agency for Education 2016, 27.)

Changing the present operational culture may be the most important and at the same time the hardest task when dealing with the development of the school. Organizations tend to be conservative and traditional by nature, and they usually encourage using strategies that strengthen the present state of issues.

• • •

Changing the present operational culture may be the most important task when dealing with the development of the school.

• • •

Furthermore, teachers as individuals are very different according to their age, experience, mindset, education, and preferences. How to fit them smoothly together in the same school? Creating a shared operational culture becomes the key issue.

Developing the operational culture is about creating shared, constructive meanings. People create meanings, either consciously or subconsciously, about different occurrences around them. When these meanings are mutual and mainly positive by nature, it becomes easier for the individuals to act and collaborate together. Shared knowledge will rise from the network of interpretations which is based on many personal things, but mainly on the present culture. The longer people immerse themselves in the culture, the more invisible it becomes. To put it simple: the more positive, open and flexible operational culture, the more constructive meanings will be selected.

How to make positive impact in the operational culture?

Principals have an important role in creating and developing an operational culture at school. Principals can, through their own behavior and actions, influence the school's operational culture. Even though the operational culture can be a complex phenomenon and concept, it can be affected in many simple ways. As a principal, these are some of the practical actions worth paying attention to:

1. Setting an example

It is not a new phenomenon that if you smile to people, sooner or later they will smile back at you. Leadership does not require status, office or uniform. Leadership only needs someone to show the way essentially anytime and anywhere. Everyday school life has tens, even hundreds of situations where someone gets the role to lead the group. Those are the key moments of effecting on the operational culture. The leader's behavior will be interpreted and partly copied in multiple situations, so make sure you model appropriate behaviors!

2. Noticing and listening

People are usually not afraid of leaders or being told what to do; they are afraid of not being respected or trusted. The easiest way to show respect is to notice individuals and to be able to arrange time, even a small slot, for them to build mutual trust – just as we act in our classroom with pupils. When we are having respectful social interaction, it is very important to also hear the things that are unspoken. Sometimes it needs to be asked if there is something else that is bothering in addition to what is said aloud. Improving and managing the message flow will also give people the feeling that they are being treated well.

3. Reacting, taking action

People always contact you for a reason. Contacting you is a sign of trust, or it could mean that people just want you to react and take some kind of action. We should always remember that from the teacher's point of view, not reacting is also an active choice made by their leader. There are cases when it is important to stop the motion and stand still for a while, but most of the time the leader should react somehow and maybe take some course of action. If you simply do not have time at the moment, just thanking for the information and telling them that you will get back to it as soon as you can is usually enough.

4. Fostering openness

Openness is in many ways the key factor to constructive operational culture. Openness has various dimensions:

- Openness for staff members to participate in any discussion or decision affecting them will improve transparency and implement trust. At the same time, people will be updated on the current issues and you can make sure that necessary information gets delivered.
- Openness to diversity will help gain deeper understanding and an enriched knowledge base for decision-making.
- Openness to conflicts in a healthy way leads to stronger solutions even in complex issues.
- Openness to reflection will help our own and others' thinking achieve better organizational decisions.
- Openness to making mistakes will allow and encourage experimentation and different experiences and simultaneously enable the learning process for all of us.

References

Finnish National Agency for Education 2016. *National core curriculum for basic education 2014.* Publications 2016:5. Helsinki.

Northouse, P. G. 2007. *Leadership theory and practice.* 4th ed. Thousand Oaks: Sage Publications.

4.3

SHARED LEADERSHIP AND TEAM ORGANIZATION IN FINNISH SCHOOLS

Jukka Miettunen (M.Ed.), Principal, Yli-Ii comprehensive school (grades K–9), Oulu, Finland
Tommi Roininen (M.Sc.), Assistant principal, Hakkari lower secondary school (grades 7–9), Lempäälä, Finland

Finnish schools have great autonomy to decide what kind of shared leadership model would benefit them the most. Therefore, different schools can have different solutions for it. In this chapter two different examples of shared leadership models from two different Finnish schools are discussed.

Example 1: Yli-Ii School (grades K–9)

Shared leadership is quite a new way of leading Finnish schools. About 10 years ago, there was only one principal in school who was responsible for everything, and all the teachers had similar tasks and responsibilities. Most principals were not accustomed or ready to delegate their responsibilities, and on the other hand, delegation was not supported by the collective labor agreement. The world and school were changing rapidly, and something had to be done to ease everyday work and pressure in all levels.

Today most of the schools in Finland, especially all the big schools, have their own shared leadership model.

The most used model is a team-based leadership. An example of the first wave five years ago is when our school organized a hackathon, where we collected all the tasks teachers and staff were obliged to do at school and wrote them on post-it labels. Because the size of our school (300 students and 30 staff persons) allows us to have four teams and team leaders, we distributed the tasks into four categories. We established teams like the pedagogical team, ICT and learning environments team, well-being team and event organizing team.

We also got resources to hire an assistant principal, who was one of our teachers. The assistant principal was paid some extra and he had four lessons less to teach than before. He was responsible for school security, the common development together with the principal, and recruiting substitute teachers. The principal, assistant principal and team leaders formed a leadership team, which had a meeting twice a month for preparing and planning developing tasks to help everyday schoolwork. This was the first opportûnity for teachers to take defined responsibilities and develop their own leadership skills. This kind of system served our school for four years. Some bigger schools also have planning groups in addition to the leadership team.

The extensive development work and projects in STEAM, learning technologies, new curriculum with transversal skills, working methods, co-teaching and teachers' co-operation all led to a lack of common planning time. Therefore, we decided to reorganize teams closer to pedagogical work and students' life. Now all teams are pedagogical teams:

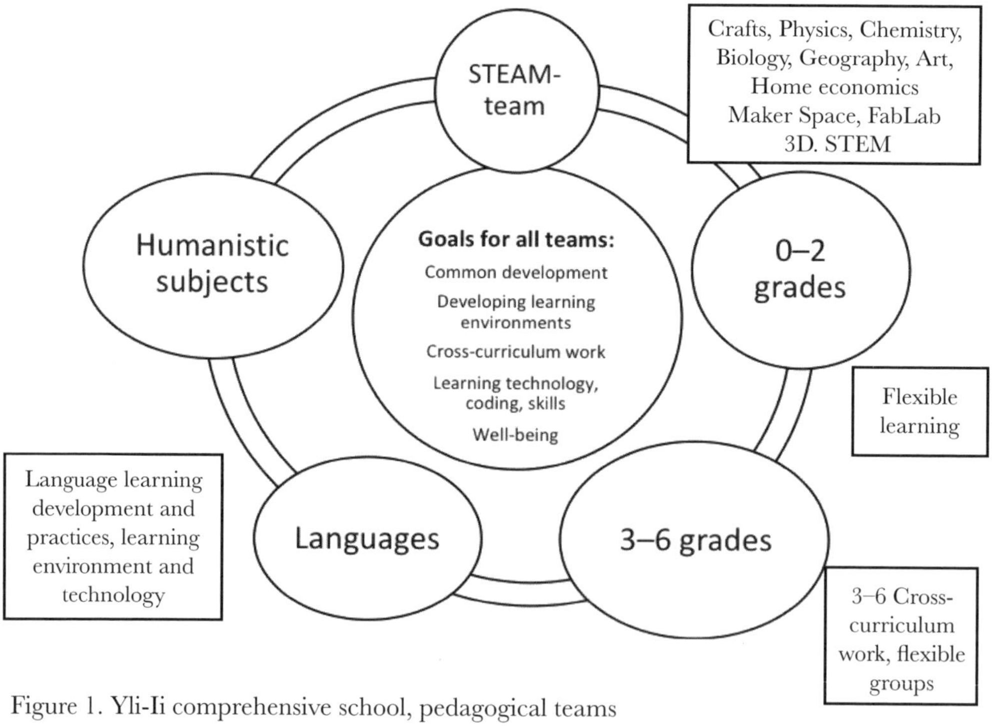

Figure 1. Yli-Ii comprehensive school, pedagogical teams

Our teams are:

1. STEAM team. All STEAM subject teachers. Responsible for enhancing STEAM-education and STEAM-path in curriculum. Taking care of our STEAM learning environment and technology.
2. Grades 0–2 team. Developing flexible learning for students aged 6–8 years.
3. Grades 3–6 team. Co-operation and multi-disciplinary projects for students aged 9–12 years.
4. Language team. Developing language education and learning environments. Global projects.
5. Humanistic subjects. Finnish language, history, student counseling.

All teams share the common developing task for the whole school, like well-being, use of learning technology, learning environments and so on. The leadership team meets twice a month as it did before.

In addition to this, we have many tasks of additional compensation for individual teachers concerning our school's emphasis areas like well-being, Schools on the move -project, IT maintenance, recycling, library, music and learning technology. Teachers are responsible for the implementation and development of the above-mentioned activities.

We are quite satisfied with our team-based leadership model and its resources. The team-based leadership model helps the school operate smoothly: every vital task has a responsible person or team. All the tasks are based on school strategy and short and long-term goals. These goals are familiar to all staff members. The principal has more time for pedagogical leadership and focusing on the big picture and strategy.

I believe that this model is suitable for schools under 500 students; bigger ones have more assistant principals and more complex team structures to serve the schoolwork. The bigger the school gets, the greater its need for precise logbooks and descriptions of everyone's responsibilities and tasks.

Example 2: Hakkari School (grades 7–9)

Trust seems to be an unexplained phenomenon inside the Finnish education system. It is hard to comprehend why our system is so heavily trust-based, and how this trust is created among different actors. One piece of the puzzle may be the shared responsibility, which is distributed among various staff teams, and thereby finally shared on an individual level. Involving staff in the planning and decision-making encourages co-operation, transparency and thinking more outside the box.

Every school community in Finland creates its own leadership model and organization structure that work for them. Our school, Hakkari school for the grades 7–9, has about 650 pupils, 60 teachers and 8 school assistants at the moment. Here is the structure of our school organization and how it works:

The core leading group

The core leading group in our school consists of the principal, the assistant principal and two vice principals. The principal acts as an immediate superior of the teachers, and the assistant principal is that of the school assistants. Most of the administrational tasks can and will be divided between the principal and assistant principal based on their personal fields of expertise and commonly negotiated details. For example, when preparing the schedules for the whole school, the principal will plan course placement, groups and teachers in the draft timetable, and the assistant principal will then add classrooms, recess supervision duties and school lunch rotation into the draft. There are also leadership tasks that cannot be divided between the principal and assistant principal, but both principals are responsible for them according to the legislation.

The vice principals are subject teachers who can have some minor administrational duties such as planning and scheduling events, acting as members of the core leading group and substitute for the principals while both of them are away from the school.

On Friday mornings, 3 times a month on average, the group meets at the principal's office for one hour to discuss upcoming and past event, and the situation at school. The group also plans some of the agenda for core school development group meetings and for our various staff teams.

The core development group

The core development group includes the chairpersons of each development team. This group gets together once a month for one hour. It plans some of the agenda for the inclusive staff meeting and operates as the main communication channel between the core leading group and the personnel. Therefore, it can make decisions more transparently and delegate tasks for the teams.

The base staff teams

All teachers belong to three different teams, and one of the members in each team acts as the chairperson to ensure the smooth operation of the group. The base teams form the backbone of communication and enable smoother information flow to all directions. They also enable more open-minded brainstorming and versatile reflective actions, for instance. There are three types of teams: subject teams, grade level teams and development teams.

The subject teams can plan, share, and develop their material, ideas, expertise, and co-operation. The grade level teams have duties related to organizing certain school celebrations along with the grade level related content, such as multidisciplinary learning modules. Usually it is the group tutors (teachers responsible for one class) who form grade level teams.

The third type of staff teams is the school-specific development teams. The staff together with the principle can decide which kind of development teams should be formed. Development teams can be, for example, teams for internationalization, curriculum, assessment, sustainable future, outdoor learning and IT. Each staff member selects one of the teams based on their expertise and interest. However, the teams should consist of teachers that represent different subjects and different grade levels. The more heterogenous the teams, the more diverse the results.

Inclusive staff meeting

All members of our pedagogical staff participate in our staff meetings. There are 10 to 15 staff meetings during the school year. Since about 70 people participate in the meetings, it is pretty obvious that there is no time for deep conversations, and the agenda has to be sufficiently simple and clear. The purpose of the staff meeting is more to inform and share rather than to have a thorough conversation and make fundamental decisions.

5

FINNISH EARLY CHILDHOOD EDUCATION AS A FOUNDATION FOR THE LIFE-LONG LEARNING PATH

Päivi Valtonen (Lic.Ed.), Pedagogical Specialist, Learning Scoop, Tampere, Finland

Early childhood education is an integral part of the success story of Finnish education. Early childhood education and care, pre-primary education and primary education form a continuum that supports the child's development and learning. Early childhood education builds a foundation for the life-long learning path in Finland.

We have high-quality early childhood education and care (ECEC) in Finland. Early childhood education is provided for children aged 0–5 years. Pre-primary education is compulsory for children of the age of six. The Finnish ECEC is based on the educare model: an integration of care, education, and teaching. The objectives, principles and contents of ECEC are guided by the National Curriculum Guidelines on ECEC, which aims to promote the provision of ECEC on equal terms throughout the country (National Core Curriculum for Early Childhood Education and Care 2017).

Finnish early childhood education has undergone interesting development processes. National Curriculum Guidelines on ECEC were released for the first time in 2017. In Finland, the municipalities are responsible for arranging ECEC services, whereas the National Core Curriculum is a legally binding regulation for ECEC providers. The local day-care personnel reflects and plans what the new guidelines mean in everyday life in the day-care centers and how they can be implemented.

Finland has, for a long time, had a strong emphasis on "stress-free childhood". Early childhood education is informal, full of play and activities that are characteristic of children, and not school-like at all. Despite of this non-formal approach, Finnish early childhood education guarantees children excellent learning abilities. How is it done and where is Finland heading next in ECEC?

Each child as a unique and valuable person

Finnish education path is, in a way, an integral entity – the same principles follow throughout the whole journey from early childhood education to basic education and to higher education, even to adult education. In every step of the education path, the learner is seen as a holistic human being, whose well-being and development as a whole person is essential. The task of early childhood education and care is to promote children's holistic growth, development and learning, health and well-being (National Core Curriculum for Early Childhood Education and Care 2017, 25).

Finnish early childhood education follows the Act on Early Childhood Education and Care and the UN Convention on the Rights of the Child. Each child is seen as an individual and a unique person. Every child is therefore valuable just as they are. The National Core Curriculum for Early Childhood Education and Care states that each child has the right to be heard, seen, noticed, and understood as themselves (National Core Curriculum for Early Childhood Education and Care 2017, 35). The main goal is to make sure that all children are happy and responsible individuals.

Early childhood education and care promotes the democratic values of Finnish society, such as equity, equality and diversity. Equity and equality are the fundamental rights of every child: all children must be treated equally and individually as their own person.

The child as an active agent

Finnish early childhood education and care implements child-centered pedagogy. It is based on the constructivist way of learning. Child-centered pedagogy focuses on children's needs and interests; the child is seen as an active agent who has the right to learn things according to their own potential.

The task of early childhood education and care is to promote children's holistic growth, development and learning, health and well-being.

The most important tools for educators are observation and listening to children. Educators listen closely to children's aspirations, ideas, wishes and questions, and they offer children possibilities to learn according to their own interests and abilities. (National Core Curriculum for Early Childhood Education and Care 2017, 70, 74.)

The Finnish conception of early childhood education is constructivist: children are seen as active agents who construct their own knowledge. Therefore, knowledge is not transferred as such; children build, or construct, it themselves. Previous knowledge, perceptions and experiences are important in learning new things. Children do not approach new things with an "empty mind", but instead are guided by their previous knowledge, perceptions and experiences of the subject matter in what they perceive and how they interpret it. New experiences gained through play and other activities are an important part of learning.

One of the central ideas of the constructivist conception of learning is that social interaction plays an important role in learning. Children learn things from each other and adults through interaction. Other people are a remarkable source of learning. Playing, discussing and engaging with others, comparing different views and exprcssing their own thoughts help children process things more deeply and from multiple perspectives. In addition, children learn social skills and work constructively with a wide variety of people. According to a study done by Jones, Greenberg and Crowley (2015), social skills learned as a child have a major impact on later life and coping with life. Interaction with peers teaches children to become more aware and responsive to their own emotional reactions and to develop problem-solving skills related to interaction (Jones, Greenberg & Crowley 2015).

Lautela (2011) has stated that child-centeredness is a response to the child's developmental stage: knowing the child's development and supporting the child according to their developmental age is a part of child-centered pedagogy. Adults' role is to support and nurture the learning process. Adults in the early childhood education unit act as facilitators who enable the child to grow, develop and learn. Adults' sensitivity is essential: their comfort, encouragement, and responsiveness to children's needs. If adults support and supervise the child's learning and individual development, the important and interesting question is, how far a child actually can go in their learning.

Key Principles of Finnish Early Childhood Education

Three central themes arise from the Finnish early childhood education guidelines: play, participation and co-operation.

Play

In Finnish early childhood education and care, learning is a continuous, everyday process. Adults along with the children's group and learning environments form the most important basis that enables the child's learning. Play is the most important way of learning in early childhood education and care. Children have the right to play, learn by playing and experience the joy of learning. Play combines the key elements that promote learning: enthusiasm, doing things together and challenging one's personal abilities.

The importance of play may be disregarded, and play may be considered "mere play". According to the constructivist conception of learning, children learn through play: they learn a wide range of skills, develop their social abilities, imagination and creativity.

Play, therefore, is not just for passing the time. It is a pedagogical activity that promotes children's development, learning and overall well-being. Often, for the child, play is not a tool for learning, but a natural way of being, acting, perceiving, and interpreting the world around them. Educators have the opportunity to use play as a pedagogical tool: they can intentionally create play settings or learning environments which aim at advancing the child's learning. Adults must also ensure that enough time is reserved, within the everyday activities of the day care, for longer play (Lastentarhanopettajaliitto ry 2004).

There are many different ways in which the constructivist conception of learning is realized in play. When playing, children are active agents who structure and explore things and the world around them, build social relationships and gain meaningful learning experiences. Play is an activity where children can combine new knowledge with previous knowledge and

Children have the right to play, learn by playing and experience the joy of learning.

thus build their own new understanding of things. Interaction also plays an important role in play, whether it is spontaneous play, guided activity or play with other children and educators.

There are many other benefits of play besides learning skills and developing social abilities, imagination and creativity:

- During play, children use skills that will enable them to meet the future challenges of daily life. Once children become aware of their own skills, they are also able to assess their own limits.
- Play helps children identify and express their own feelings. Play generates emotional experiences, like joy and sorrow, success and disappointment, excitement, and calmness.
- Playing in itself creates positivity and joy in children, in groups and in the whole learning community. Play brings a positive atmosphere to the group that is a good starting point for all activities and learning.

Play can take many forms and unfold in many different contexts and learning environments: indoors, in the yard, in the immediate surroundings, in the playground, on the sports field or in the woods. Play can also be made up of different physical activities. In Finnish Early Childhood Education, physical activity plays an important role because it is one of the characteristics of children, just as play is. According to studies, physical activity has a positive effect on children's learning and their overall well-being (Syväoja, Kantomaa, Laine, Jaakkola, Pyhältö & Tammelin 2012).

Nature, especially the forest, is also an important part of the early childhood education environment. In nature, children have the opportunity to learn everyday skills and general knowledge. Nature is also a good place for environmental education: children can be taught responsible action in the environment as well as the basics of sustainable living. In addition, children can learn skills such as mathematical thinking in nature, like in the forest. Mathematical thinking can be practiced, for example, by observing numbers in the environment: how many trees or rocks are in a certain area, how many petals different forest wildflowers have or how many seeds are in a mountain ash berry. Children can try measurement: how can their arms reach around a tree, or how many steps are needed to get from one tree to the other.

In addition to playing and moving, wondering, and exploring are among natural ways for the child to be. There are many things to observe in nature: the soil, plants, trees, rocks, lights and shadows, and sounds. In addition, nature can enhance children's geometric thinking in different ways, such as by studying pieces and shapes, or practicing spatial concepts. Children can become familiar with the concept of time by observing the seasons and times of day: how the nearby forest changes from season to season, or whether it is different in the morning and afternoon. If adults do not discover anything to explore outside, children will! Trips in the local surroundings can inspire children to come up with exciting phenomenological projects just by chance.

The forest is a versatile learning environment full of play supplies (rocks, sticks, pinecones, and other natural materials) and imagination stimulating elements, shapes and colors. Another great thing about the adaptable forest environment is that play in the forest is often shared and not gender specific. In the forest, children can find common interests and their collective positive experiences reinforce their feeling of belonging to the group.

The forest promotes the overall well-being of both adults and children. The mind becomes peaceful and relaxed in the forest, and heart rate, blood pressure and stress are reduced. Moving and playing in such a varied landscape are among the best outdoor and physical activities for children. Studies indicate that positive effects occur already within 15 minutes of being in the forest (Tyrväinen, Sievänen, Tuulentie & Kurttila 2014).

In Finland, many early childhood education units are situated close to a forest and have a free access to it, but of course not all units have this. Any nearby environment, such as a yard, a park, a beach, or a green space can be used instead. What is important is to realize that learning does not have to just occur within the four walls of the classroom.

Play is significant for learning, but children also learn by moving, exploring, working on different assignments, and expressing themselves artistically. The starting point for pedagogical activities in early childhood education is children's natural ways of being and acting.

Participation

In the National Core Curriculum for Early Childhood Education and Care (2017), the children's participative role increases. Children's participation is understood to include aspects such as

- having opportunities to influence their learning and the culture of kindergartens,
- having opportunities to plan, implement and evaluate activities,
- being respected and listened to by educators, and

- having chances to practice responsibility and self-regulation (Kangas 2016, 59–64).

Participation is not just about involvement, it is about the feeling of being a part of a community and being able to be heard, express yourself and take initiatives (Weckström, Jääskeläinen, Ruokonen, Karlsson & Ruismäki 2017).

Practical issues affect participation. For example, the size of the daycare groups has to be reasonable so that children's participation can be achieved in the best possible way.

The Early Childhood Education Act (Varhaiskasvatuslaki 2015) stipulates that a group can host a combined maximum number of children corresponding to three early childhood education staff members. In practice, this means that in a group of over three-year-old children can be a maximum of 21 children.

The role of educators as facilitators of children's participation is considered essential. A precondition for children's participation is that adults are genuinely present, listen to the children, and are sensitive to their messages, observe them, and strive to reach the children's perspective. (National Core Curriculum for Early Childhood Education and Care 2017, 57–58, 74). Adults have the power to influence the involvement of children and to decide whether and to what extent children's thoughts and views are considered.

Turja states that hearing children is not just taking notice of individual children's thoughts and perspectives, but instead noting those of the whole group, taking different perspectives into consideration, fitting them together and finding a solution that satisfies everyone. Therefore, children's participation is also considered collective action. A shared decision can be reached for example by voting and negotiating in the group (Turja 2011, 30). These activities are also partly pedagogical activities which guide children towards learning democratic procedures. At the end of the day, the purpose of participation is for children to develop into active and responsible actors within the Finnish democratic society.

Co-operation

Participation and collaboration in early childhood education does not only concern children, but their guardians as well. According to the Finnish Early Childhood Education Act (2015), the guardian has to be given the opportunity to participate and affect the planning, implementation and evaluation of their child's early childhood education. Successful collaboration between parents and personnel brings continuity and security in the children's lives (National Core Curriculum for Early Childhood Education and Care 2017, 33).

Participation and collaboration between the guardians and the daycare staff can be multilayered and multifaceted. Both can be accomplished through brief daily conversations when the parent brings or comes to collect the child from the daycare. Participation and collaboration can also be more organized and planned: they can be carried out through the Parents' Association. One of its objectives is to promote the interaction between parents, which occurs at these association activities. The networking and collaboration of parents strengthens the sense of community and supports the daycare personnel's work.

Open discussion sessions and parent-teacher evenings can also be organized; parents can brainstorm and plan the daycare's activities and operation with the personnel. Furthermore, designing the child's individual plan is also a collaborative effort. Discussions based on a written or electronic plan create a peaceful interactive situation between the parents and the daycare personnel.

What is essential is that the daycare personnel offers parents different opportunities to participate and to collaborate while taking families' life situations and possibilities to participate into consideration. Parents can decide for themselves when they want to participate and influence decisions, as well as how active they want to be in the collaboration.

The general objectives of Early Childhood Education

There are no academic objectives set in Finnish early childhood education. Children do not have to learn letters or numbers, let alone reading, counting, or participating in any other knowledge-based teaching. Early childhood education is nothing like school: children do not have subjects, classes, textbooks, or exams. Their day is mostly made up of care, play and group activities in a variety of learning environments. The day's schedule can be very open and can include outdoor activities, handicrafts, guided or free play, and naturally care, meals and rest.

National Core Curriculum for Early Childhood Education and Care (2017) set general objectives, or in other words, transversal competencies. They answer the question of what kind of knowledge will be required in society and working life in the future. Therefore, children are being raised and taught to respond to the challenges of the future.

The Finnish National Agency for Education (Rinkinen 2014) has described the kind of future citizens that Finland needs as

- active and innovative,
- committed to their community and willing to work together,
- international and multilingual,
- creative and able to adapt their know-how,
- critical and analytical thinkers,
- generalists and lifelong learners,
- believers in the future and oneselves, and
- interactive and collaborative.

The development of the aforementioned skills and characteristics is believed to begin in early childhood and to continue throughout life. They strengthen along the path of growth and learning, as well as through day-to-day activity and interaction. Knowledge, skills, values, attitudes, and will form the whole of transversal competencies.

Transversal competencies are

- thinking and learning
- cultural competence, interaction and self-expression
- taking care of oneself and managing daily life
- multiliteracy and competence in information and communication technology
- participation and involvement (National Core Curriculum for Early Childhood Education and Care 2017).

Thinking and learning

Thinking and learning skills form the foundation for the development of other competences and life-long learning. Those skills are developed in interaction with other people. In carly childhood education, variety, and creative activities (such as music, artistic expression and drama) as well as play develop thinking and learning-to-learn skills. Also, the possibility to express oneself and one's own perspectives, and the opportunity to ask and question have a positive effect on the development of a child's thinking skills (National Core Curriculum for Early Childhood Education and Care 2017, 44–45).

Cultural competence, interaction, and self-expression

The world is culturally, linguistically and religiously diverse. The educator's task is to help children form a positive relationship with it. Interactive skills and the ability to express oneself and to understand others is practiced in the group with peers as well as adults during play, visits, and field trips, and during celebrations and other events (National Core Curriculum for Early Childhood Education and Care 2017, 45–46).

Taking care of oneself and managing daily life

The task of early childhood education and care is to strengthen children's skills related to well-being and safety. The gradual increase in the children's level of independence is supported by giving them the opportunity to practice getting dressed, eating, and taking care of their own hygiene. Children are also given the opportunity to handle small tasks as well as to help others. As a part of well-being, children are taught emotional skills; in other words, they are guided to recognize and to name their own feelings. The educator's task is to ensure that the day's program is suitable for children: the child has to have enough opportunities for rest, healthy eating as well as play and outdoor activity (National Core Curriculum for Early Childhood Education and Care 2017, 46–47).

Multiliteracy and competence in information and communication technology

Multiliteracy refers to skills of interpreting and producing various types of messages. Multiliteracy comprises different types of literacy, such as visual literacy, numerical literacy, media literacy and basic literacy. Children are encouraged to explore, use, and produce messages in different environments. They are also exposed to different kinds of information and communications technology equipment, services, and games. The main objective for using information and communications technology is to support the development of expression, learning and interaction of children (National Core Curriculum for Early Childhood Education and Care 2017, 47–48).

Participation and involvement

Children have the opportunity to plan, implement and assess activity together with other children, as well as adults. Participation and involvement develop a child's interactive skills as well as help them to perceive the meaning of collective rules, agreements, and trust. The educator's role is to listen to the children's wishes and needs, to observe children, to plan activities together with them as well as to support and encourage children. Children also gain confidence by helping each other and by asking for help when needed (National Core Curriculum for Early Childhood Education and Care 2017, 48–49).

Learning areas promote transversal competencies

In National Core Curriculum for Early Childhood Education and Care, the central themes in planning and implementing pedagogical activities are called learning areas. Transversal competencies form the general objectives of early childhood activity: their purpose is to indicate what kind of knowledge, know-how and skills children should have in the future. The learning areas contain themes that educators can use in their daily work, and which in part help attain the objectives of the transversal competencies. Using the themes and activities set out in the learning areas promotes the development of children's transversal competencies.

Learning area themes can be used in all early childhood education activities, for example in different group situations and events, during play and also during care. Children's interests and needs are taken into consideration with the themes as well, and the activities can be planned together with the children. The role of the educator is to ensure that the pedagogical activity gives children of all ages the opportunity to try, practice, teach and learn using new skills at their own pace within all the learning areas.

The learning areas are:
- Rich world of languages
- Diverse forms of expression
- Me and our community
- Exploring and interacting with my environment
- I grow, move and develop (National Core Curriculum for Early Childhood Education and Care 2017, 79).

Rich world of languages

Children's interest in languages, and especially in their own mother tongue, is awakened in early childhood education. This happens through rhyming and language play activities among others. Children can make up their own stories, plays, rhymes, and so on. Language development is supported through the educator's linguistic modeling, educators and children reading together and leisurely conversations between them. Educators pay attention to how the child's actions are guided through language and are verbalized, particularly in daily situations and play (National Core Curriculum for Early Childhood Education and Care 2017, 80–83).

Diverse forms of expression

In early childhood education, children can experiment with and practice their musical, visual, verbal, and physical expression, as well as learn basic skills in handiwork. Musical expression is taught through learning songs, listening to music, becoming familiar with different music styles and instruments, producing music as well as through dance and movement with music. With visual expression, children have the opportunity to try different ways, tools and materials for making pictures. Visual expression also includes interpreting and critiquing art. During crafting activity, children experiment how different materials are used and practice the techniques needed to work with those materials. (National Core Curriculum for Early Childhood Education and Care 2017, 83–87.)

Me and our community

In early childhood education, children understand that there are many types of societies and families, and there are many ways of thinking and acting. Children are guided towards positive interaction. Children work in different groups and in pairs. They learn to work with different people and have the opportunity to practice their social skills. Furthermore, group rules are considered together and built collectively. (National Core Curriculum for Early Childhood Education and Care 2017, 87–89.)

In addition, children also learn to constructively resolve different conflict situations. Many Finnish daycares use a peer mediation program, where children's conflicts are resolved by themselves: the parties of the dispute are helped to find their own solution to the problem by using a specific action model. The parties express their viewpoint of the problem, their feelings, and their thoughts on various solutions. The goal is to reduce conflicts as well as to learn interactive and problem-solving skills. (Gellin 2017.)

Exploring and interacting with my environment

Learning in early childhood education is based on the premise of working and acting together. By doing so, children gain individual, positive learning experiences that produce the joy of discovery and learning. Situations where children can learn things, such as mathematical thinking, are created through play-like activity. The starting point for the activity is that learning occurs in a variety of daily situations and in different learning environments. For example, nature and field trips carry special meaning in Finnish early childhood education. Moving around and working in nature provides the best environmental education available. Learning does not happen by transferring knowledge to children, but through encouraging them to experiment and to observe, as well as to ask questions and to find answers to those questions together. (National Core Curriculum for Early Childhood Education and Care 2017, 89–93.)

I grow, move and develop

The goal of ECEC is to inspire children to be physically active in a variety of ways, as well as to discover the joy of it. Physical activity promotes learning and is otherwise important for a child's overall well-being and development. Early childhood education units use physical activity in both inside and outside environments, and children's wishes, and interests are taken into consideration. Physical activity can include different games, such as ball, yard, story, and musical games. In winter, activities can also include snow games, skating and skiing. (National Core Curriculum for Early Childhood Education and Care 2017, 93–94.)

From a child's well-being standpoint, regularly scheduled meals are important. Dining situations are a part of nutritional education; the goal is to create a positive relationship with food and eating, as well as to support a well-balanced eating habit. Dining occurs at a relaxed pace, without forcing or pressuring children to eat. At the same time, children learn good table manners and a culture of eating together. Dining situations provide the children the opportunity to participate and to learn daily skills. Children can, among other things, set the table, serve themselves and portion the food, separate the trash and recyclable leftovers and clean the dining area. (National Core Curriculum for Early Childhood Education and Care 2017, 94–95.)

Children's natural ways of acting develop readiness for learning

In Finland, a new early childhood education and care curriculum took effect on 1 August 2017. Before that, many ECEC units were already implementing the main pillars of the curriculum. Play, participation and working together were already the cornerstones of Finnish ECEC and units were already using a plethora of good, curriculum-based activities and procedures. According to ECEC personnel, the only difference between the new curriculum and the previous one is that the guidelines for ECEC plans are now written as 'a policy document' that obligates action according to the document.

The ECEC guidelines are not only a binding administrative document, but also a child-centered pedagogical handbook; it explains what kind of early childhood education Finnish children have the right to. The central idea of the ECEC guidelines is that children can have a stress-free childhood and can truly and freely be children. The guidelines set out objectives for early childhood education operations, not for children. Children's learning is not measured or assessed; the assessment is focused on early childhood education activities, arrangement, learning environments and pedagogy.

Finnish ECEC is authentically child-centered action. Children can act in their specific way: playing, moving, wondering and asking, examining, and expressing themselves artistically. All the above-mentioned ways of acting develop the child's readiness for learning. The role of the educator is to offer children the most varied opportunities for different activities as possible, adapt the day care environment to suit the child's needs, and support the child age-appropriately in various actions.

Studies show that pre-primary aged children or younger are not ready for school-like activities. School-like routines and too high expectations from an age perspective can even hinder the child's development. (Katz 2015, Lautela 2011.)

Furthermore, Katz has stated that children learn best in informal and interactive situations. For this reason, children should be offered broadly different opportunities and situations that produce learning experiences for them. Neurological research does not imply that formal academic teaching and instruction are the way to optimize early brain development. In contrast, academic objectives should be forgotten when considering small children (objectives such as focusing on knowledge-based learning, and teaching reading and writing); the focus should be shifted to developing thinking skills (questioning, thinking, decision-making and analyzing among others), social skills and emotional skills instead. Research indicates that formal academic teaching makes children passive, and this has been proven to be detrimental to children's intellectual growth. Formal academic teaching is even more damaging to boys than to girls. (Katz 2015.)

In Finland, ECEC gives every child the space and the opportunity to develop their own thinking, interactive, collaborative and emotional skills. The best foundation for learning comes from giving children the opportunity to develop in peace.

The best foundation for learning comes from giving children the opportunity to develop in peace.

References

Gellin, M. 2017. *The VERSO programme in Finland. Towards Restorative Learning Communities – Mediation in the field of Education*. Finnish Forum for Meditation.

Jones, D. E., Greenberg, M., & Crowley, M. 2015. Early Social-Emotional Functioning and Public Health: The Relationship Between Kindergarten Social Competence and Future Wellness. *American Journal of Public Health 105, 11*, 2283–2290.

Kangas, J. 2016. *Enhancing children's participation in early childhood education through the participatory pedagogy*. Academic dissertation. University of Helsinki, Faculty of Behavioral Science, Department of Teacher Education.

Katz, L. 2015. *Lively Minds: Distinctions between academic versus intellectual goals for young children.* Defending the Early Years. DEY.

Lautela, R. 2011. Esiopetuksen lähtökohtia [The baseline of pre-primary education]. In Jantunen, T., & Lautela, R. (Eds.) *Lapsilähtöinen esiopetus* [Child-centered pre-primary education] Helsinki: SanomaPro, 31–35.

Lastentarhanopettajaliitto ry [Kindergarten/Early childhood education teacher's union of Finland]. 2004. *Leikin aika*. Lastentarhanopettajaliiton julkaisu [The time of the play. Publication by the Kindergarten/Early childhood education teacher's union of Finland].

National Core Curriculum for Early Childhood Education and Care 2016. 2017. Finnish National Agency for Education. Regulations and guidelines 10. Helsinki.

Rinkinen, A. 2014. *Ajankohtaista yleissivistävän koulutuksen kehittämisessä* [Recent developments in comprehensive education]. Helsinki: Opetushallitus [Finnish National Agency for Education].

Syväoja, H., Kantomaa, M., Laine, K., Jaakkola, T., Pyhältö, K., & Tammelin, T. 2012. *Liikunta ja oppiminen* [Movement and learning]. Opetushallituksen tilannekatsaus [A review of the current situation by the Finnish National Agency for Education]. Muistiot [Notes] 5. Helsinki: Opetushallitus [Finnish National Agency for Education].

Turja, L. 2011. Lapset osallisina – kohti uutta varhaiskasvatuskulttuuria [Children as partners – towards a new early childhood education culture]. *Varhaiskasvatus ry:n verkkolehti*

[Online journal of the Finnish early childhood education association], toukokuu [May] 2011, 24–35.
Tyrväinen, L., Sievänen, T., Tuulentie, S., & Kurttila, M. (Eds.) 2014. *Hyvinvointia metsästä* [Wellbeing from nature]. Helsinki: SKS.
Varhaiskasvatuslaki [Act on Early childhood education and care]. 2015. 5 a § (8.5.2015).
Weckström, E., Jääskeläinen, V., Ruokonen, I., Karlsson, L., & Ruismäki, H. 2017. Steps together: Children's experiences of participation in club activities with the elderly. *Journal of Intergenerational Relationships 3, 15*, 273–289.

5.1

EDUCATING THE WHOLE CHILD: GETTING THE BALANCE RIGHT

Elena Chukhlantseva (M.Ed.), ECEC Specialist, Learning Scoop, Tampere, Finland

It is so exciting to live in the age of neuroscience! A growing body of brain research is just impressive. However, single research findings as such cannot provide straightforward answers as to how to raise and educate children. To have practical value, research work is carried out and interpreted at the intersection with other sciences to build a better understanding of the child.

In the education field these days, we are invigorating the discussion about the whole child or whole-brain child perspective. The primary question is how to help and support the child's brain to grow towards *integration* to make a well-functioning whole – a healthy, happy and learning child. We talk about integration within and between various parts of the brain, the integration of mental, physical, social and emotional dimensions in self, and the integration of self and the other.

In fact, the whole child or whole-brain child perspective is not novel. At least since the age of ancient Greece in western history, we have had a rich heritage of philosophical, theoretical, and experimental work that provides us with valuable insights on the value of childhood and the child's development. What makes the whole-brain approach to education particularly topical today is the additional light that neuroscience sheds on what has been previously thought, debated, and put into practice.

The interest in the whole child approach strongly resonates with the increasing concern among professionals in many countries about a narrow understanding of what 'readiness to learn' and 'school readiness' mean. Inappropriate expectations for the child, prevalence of drilling academic skills, over-assessment and excessive pressure of competition are among recognized weaknesses in many systems. They cause disbalance in the child's whole-brain integration and have far-reaching undesirable effects on the child's motivation and interest in learning, health, and overall well-being.

There are alternatives to mere 'academic kindergartens'. They have been coined as all-round education, holistic development approach, 3H (Head-Heart-Hand) approach and integrated curriculum, among others. It would not be an exaggeration to say that what a progressive educator John Dewey (1902 7–9; 1909 96–97; 1946 186–196) formulated in his time truly grasps the essence of the concepts related to the 'whole child' approach: all parts are equally present, dependent on each other; the parts constitute and interpret the whole, similarly as the whole cannot be perceived apart from its interacting parts; subject-matter cannot be isolated from its connections, ties and consequences with respect to which it acts. Therefore, there is more to the child than their academic knowledge and performance.

In the context of Finnish early childhood education and care, we talk about the 'Educare model' based on the integrated approach to care, education and teaching. The underlying idea is to connect instead of dividing. We see the child as a unity of their mental and physical health, social-emotional functioning and development, and learning potential. Unlike schooling with the focus on academics, the Educare model contributes to the whole child's well-being by integrating various elements within the child as well as between the child and their environment. The Educare model is largely based on systematic research in developmental psychology and the socio-constructivist approach to learning.

The younger the child, the more important it is to attend to the basic necessities and to instill basic skills. Gradually teaching the principle of self-efficacy and mastery in, say, dressing, feeding, toileting, understanding and following directions, communicating, formulating questions, and thinking as well as directing one's own actions are far more essential and relevant to the young child than teaching them mastery of reading and counting numbers

We see the child as a unity of their mental and physical health, social-emotional functioning and development, and learning potential.

up to several hundreds. If we, early childhood educators, prepare children for the upcoming school years with the prevailing focus on academics, but miss to teach children everyday routines and daily life skills, then we have to honestly admit that we failed to fulfill the core task of our job.

Moreover, we do not talk about school readiness in academic terms as such in Finland; we rather turn to the psychological, personal, emotional and social foundations any learning inevitably rests on. Through nurturing the child's attitudes and dispositions, self-image and self-confidence, individual strengths, emotional and behavioral regulation, engaged action and group skills, we can best prepare the child to take on more complex and challenging tasks. Alone, these may be separate learning goals, but in addition to that they are a means to other learning and enhanced achievement across all areas of development or curriculum.

Learning brings experiences of success and joy to the child when it unfolds through play. According to Moore (2014), Rogers states that play is not a relief from serious learning. Instead, play is the highest form of research involving intense thought activity. It is the fabric into which a multitude of concepts and experiences can be woven. An imaginative play with the fight of the good and the bad teaches what is right and wrong or how to overcome fears. A constructive play introduces a variety of mathematical concepts like size, patterns, measure, and weight, and can integrate with storytelling for linguistic development. Climbing trees promotes courage and motor skills as well as extends creativity and innovation when the tree turns into a ship. Engaging in handclapping promotes phonological awareness and can also be the start for a new dance when movement is added. Children do not need to sit at their desks, not even when learning concepts of literacy and numeracy; they just need teachers who prioritize the way the child learns. Why not start with exploring concrete things in the immediate environment and, say, spot and draw items of a circle shape on a walk outdoors, or count how many steps we jump for the number of syllables in the word 'hel-lo'?

Neuroscience's claim of the brain being plastic, or moldable, only confirms that the presence – or lack – of experiences, thoughts and actions in various development areas shape the architecture and function of the brain in certain ways. To think in terms of opposites like 'one skills area over another', or 'hard skills versus soft skills' or 'learning versus play' is to steal away from children what they would otherwise enjoy as a whole experience. Ultimately, these are human choices.

References

Dewey, J. 1909. *How we think.* Reprint, US: Martino Fine Books, 2011.

Dewey, J. 1915, 1902. *The school and society; &, The child and the curriculum.* Reprint, New York: Dover Publications, 2001.

Dewey, J. 1927. *The public and its problems.* Reprint, Ohio: Swallow Press, 1991.

Moore, H. 2014. *Why play is the work of childhood.* Blog post. Accessed on 25 September 2019. Retrieved from: https://www.fredrogerscenter.org/2014/09/why-play-is-the-work-of-childhood/

5.2

PARTNERSHIP WITH FAMILIES IN EARLY CHILDHOOD EDUCATION

Elena Chukhlantseva (M.Ed.), ECEC Specialist, Learning Scoop, Tampere, Finland

Many educators from around the world come to Finland to be introduced to the Finnish Early Childhood Education and Care (ECEC) system. They experience and observe real situations and interaction among children and adults. They get very excited and overwhelmed with many thoughts and ideas they would like to have as a takeaway. We often hear that the way we work with families of young children deserves a special honour. Indeed, partnership with families is considered a priority when raising a child in Finland.

Of course, family is always a place where parents model behavior, habits, routines, attitudes, and skills to their child, and therefore it is a place for learning. Family is also a "safe harbor" where the child is unconditionally loved and gets the most attention, where their happiness and joy are shared, and where they are helped and supported through difficult moments. According to the Finnish legislation, the family carries the primary responsibility for raising the child. On the other hand, the child spends a lot of time in early childhood education settings. In fact, children in Finland spend on average eight hours a day, five days a week in day care centres while parents are at work. The child's understanding of the world around them, their place in it and the role models from home are reinforced through social interaction in a group with other children and adults. The child learns what they live and lives what they learn in both environments, home and day care. If the child experiences inconsistency in parental and day care approaches, the lesson they learn is confusion. The child is then also likely to lack the sense of security in the child-carer attachment relationship, which has a long-term impact on the child's overall well-being and learning.

Curiously enough, the Finnish language has one word for what is called in different national contexts *nursery*, *kindergarten*, *pre-school*, *child care* or other – the word is *päiväkoti*, which literally means "day home". It is quite fascinating to think that the early childhood education and care setting can be an extension of the child's home at its best!

So, how do we build a partnership with families, promote their participation in early childhood education and care of their child and advance a healthy functional relationship? Indeed, the process of collaboration requires many things, but most of all it demands the ECEC personnel and the families to make a multitude of adjustments towards the key aim: the child's balanced growth and development, holistic learning and well-being.

The starting point for collaboration with families is our common understanding that The Child is what we both hold dear! We do not need to oppose 'us' to 'them' and compete with each other about who is more important or knowledgeable. Neither will we tell each other what to do or blame each other for what failed to be achieved. Disconnected and non-convergent modes of work leave no constructive traces behind; neither do they serve the task of maximizing the child's individual potential in growth, development, and learning. We shall work for the best of the child together.

The power relations in early childhood education between families and the ECEC settings in Finland are rather in a horizontal, networking dimension where we complement and empower each other. This is enacted through open communication, continuous flow of information exchange, respecting each other, listening, and hearing each other, working towards shared meanings and understandings, designing effective practices in working with the child together and learning from each other.

In addition, The Finnish Core Curriculum for ECEC sets the framework for the process of collaboration between families and ECEC settings. There are numerous opportunities for families to participate in formulating the

The starting point for collaboration with families is our common understanding that The Child is what we both hold dear!

child's learning objectives and the adults' working methods, discussing the progress of their child, contributing to the life of the day care, educating themselves and experiencing that their opinions and ideas have an effect.

Building and constantly fine-tuning healthy relationships with families may not necessarily be a fast or easy process. It requires time, patience and commitment. However, whatever challenge or difficulty we may face, we can always choose to look at it as a new opportunity rather than an obstacle. There is little to no sense in stopping by the wall. There is a great deal of sense in making efforts and building bridges over the wall!

5.3

CHILD'S INDIVIDUAL EARLY CHILDHOOD EDUCATION AND CARE (ECEC) PLAN: NAVIGATING THE ROAD AHEAD

Elena Chukhlantseva (M.Ed.), ECEC Specialist, Learning Scoop, Tampere, Finland

There is hardly anything new in saying that children learn as individuals, learn for themselves, learn in different ways and at different rates. Children need adults to support them in maximizing their potential and to accommodate their individual needs. How can we teachers and educators cater to the diversity in children's groups? How can we provide for individual growth instead of stumbling over a 'one-size-fits-all' approach that promises easier classroom management, but in reality, squeezes children down narrow channels?

One of the well-established and valuable practices in the Finnish education system is the building of an individual path for each learner. Building the individual path is, in fact, a common thread that unites the Finnish national core curricula for education at all levels, starting from early childhood. The underlying thinking is that in the journey of lifelong learning, the person needs to follow their unique path that cannot be walked by another person.

In early childhood, we begin building the individual path by drawing up the child's Individual Early Childhood Education and Care (ECEC) Plan.

• • •

One of the well-established and valuable practices in the Finnish education system is the building of an individual path for each learner.

• • •

The Plan is designed not only for children with learning or behavioural challenges or support needs of various kinds – the Individual Plan is prepared for every child in the group so that they could have access to a meaningful curriculum and balanced social, psychological, and physical environments.

The Individual ECEC Plan is drawn up annually, usually within two months of the start of the school year, around September and October. It is a collaborative document and builds upon four perspectives:

- the National Core Curriculum for ECEC;
- the teachers and other educators' pedagogical knowledge, professional expertise and observations on central factors in the child's development, learning and well-being, and on how the child interacts in a group;
- the views and opinions of the child's guardians;
- the views and opinions of the child.

The aim of the Plan is to set shared objectives for action and agree on ways to promote the child's individual development, learning and well-being in a systematic and goal-oriented manner. This is why the Plan is a pedagogical plan in the first place and serves as a tool for designing pedagogical activity. The Plan is discussed at a pre-scheduled meeting together with the child's guardians and the child. Prior to the meeting, the teacher in cooperation with other educators and the child's guardians prepare for the discussion meeting and write their notes in the blank copies of the Individual ECEC Plan.

What is inside the Individual ECEC Plan, then? The Plan which supports the implementation of the National Core Curriculum for ECEC is not about describing what the child is like (e.g. smart, kind, aggressive), or merely ticking the child's skills in the developmental milestones chart (e.g. can balance on one foot, cannot feed self). Instead, the teacher and the child's guardians discuss the child's strengths and successes and how they are taken into consideration in terms of action.

Example: Roosa is able to recognize and name her own feelings. She has learnt a breathing technique to calm herself down whenever she feels upset or frustrated. Roosa's father tells us that she uses the technique at home too. At the day care, we take aspects of emotional competence into consideration when planning group activities.

The teachers, educators and the child's guardians closely observe the child, listen to the child and pay attention to the ideas, interests and opinions the child conveys through their actions or formulates verbally. When including the child's perspectives in the Plan, we emphasise the child's agency in learning.

Discovered strengths and interests serve as the basis for setting the objectives that are significant for the child's well-being and learning. They do not only give us information about the child's emerging skills that need advancement, but also about the child's inner resources that can be utilized in practicing new skills. Importantly, the objectives are not articulations of our expectations for the child to reach. The objectives have to specify what action the teachers, educators and child's guardians should take to support the child's development in the desired direction.

Example: Because Saara is eager to learn new words, we will help her expand her vocabulary and encourage her to use new words in relevant situations and experiences. We have agreed with her guardians that we share practical ideas and experiences with each other on a regular base.

The next step is to develop the measures and methods for achieving the objectives. They need to be motivating, engaging and relevant to the child so that the child can experience ownership of their learning and eventually feel pride in their achievements and confidence in their abilities. The methods also need to be very concrete and practical.

Example: Because Aapo needs to move a lot during the day both at home and day care, we will create him more opportunities for movement. We will combine physical activity with songs, rhymes and stories, introduce more active breaks, use movements of animals and vehicles in transition situations, integrate Aapo's good construction skills into activities like building various obstacle courses with sports equipment for others to try, move to different types of music, explore the impact of movement on health.

The Individual ECEC Plan needs to be assessed and reviewed at least once a year or whenever necessary. The initiative for the Plan review can come from the day care centre or the family. Because we set the objectives for action, we focus on assessing pedagogical activities, learning environments and other relevant arrangements, not the child. We discuss whether the measures have been realized, whether they have been functional, effective and impactful, and what new strategies, solutions or modifications to adults' action need to be considered.

The primary responsibility for the coordination of the Plan's drafting and assessment rests with the key teacher of the child. Other professionals such as a special education teacher, psychologist, occupational therapist, speech therapist, medical nurse or doctor and others join in when necessary, or when more complex support measures need to be provided to the child.

The child's Individual ECEC Plan is a powerful tool for navigating the road ahead; the road the child and the adults walk together, the road where the child is the curriculum.

5.4

CHILD'S SPACE: LET'S HAVE A LEARNING ENVIRONMENT MAKEOVER!

Elena Chukhlantseva (M.Ed.), ECEC Specialist, Learning Scoop, Tampere, Finland

Some of you might agree with me that when you have been in the teaching profession for long enough, it is a bit of a challenge to turn off the 'professional mode' after leaving the workplace. Every now and then in my free time, I catch myself observing children's play, their interaction and behavioural responses to the various emotional states they experience. Honestly speaking, I find it curious to see how children make sense of the world around, what strategies they use to engage with the environment and people, what kinds of personalities they have beyond the bounds of an organized early childhood education centre (ECEC) service, such as a day care.

I remember seeing a child leaping like a frog down the aisle in a grocery store one day. While being fully immersed in her make-believe play, she was making "ribbit" sounds and occasional movements with her head and eyes. So natural in her ways, she was communicating: "I can do, play, move, express myself at any time and in any environment."

Indeed, the immediate physical environment is a child's space. It is something that matters and provides the context for the child's ways of being, knowledge construction and skill practice. It is also one of the three dimensions of early childhood environment alongside the social and psychological ones (Core Curriculum for Early Childhood Education and Care, Finland, 2016), which altogether contribute to the child's well-being, development and learning in a complex way.

What makes the space and available physical environment a quality learning environment? The way we understand and think of the physical environment along with its educational potential and how we implement relative work practices derives from the conception of learning that we adhere to.

The importance of function, structure and arrangement of space has been appreciated and scrupulously addressed by various educational schools based on child-centred philosophy. It has been advocated that early childhood spaces need to provide for goal-oriented and purposeful engagement, interaction, inquiry, experimentation, movement, expression and so on. Indeed, a well-thought, pedagogically justified environment intentionally designed by adults is conducive to development and learning. Classroom design, toys, games, supplies and equipment which are age-appropriate and cater to the abilities of each child are crucial for advancing various skills and knowledge.

A quality physical environment is both a 'container' and 'content'. It is a medium in which the child acts and through interaction with which the child makes connections, interpretations, and meanings. The child's continuous mobility of thought and action suggests that their environment should allow for flexibility and modification. Consisting of multiple elements, objects and materials, the environment should be active and evolve along with children's needs and interests, functionality, project themes and so on.

At its best, the environment should invite children to create their own content in it! Let us consider an example: a play is unfolding among two to three-year-old children with only play silks in their hands in an almost empty room. Such an arrangement is a deliberate choice by the teachers and educators who aim to enhance children's imagination, creativity and interaction skills. A well-known Finnish principle "less is more" is well exemplified here. The environment can still be meaningful and educative without being abundant or complete or brought to perfection – it is never an end in itself.

The idea of a flexible environment does not apply to classroom arrangements only. We can discover or create the learning environment anywhere around us. A favourable physical environment should make

• • •

At its best, the learning environment should invite children to create their own content in it!

• • •

it possible to blend various learning areas and practise several skills simultaneously. We could assign a new meaning to a transition area by setting up a sensory path on the floor. We could also design a story-telling activity in a sports hall by first making a collective story, then taking out the sports equipment and thinking how to tell the story with movements and available equipment (e.g. hula hoops, balls, climbing frame, bean bags, tiles). By recognizing multiple opportunities in outdoor spaces, we can play various bingo games or design a pirates QR code track or try a compound words hunt in the day care playground or the nearby park, forest or library. Seeing familiar spaces in such ways that contribute to pedagogical action is something worthwhile teaching to ourselves.

When making choices about an environment, adults usually assess what could be useful for children. However, we should also ask children and find out what kinds of environments they find nice and comfortable, what they like the best in the day care, what opportunities different spaces provide in their eyes, and how to make children's presence and traces of daily life visible at the day care. Children are capable of giving us clues and wonderful ideas that we would either pass by or not register otherwise. The child's participation and influence, which are central values in the Finnish Core Curriculum for ECEC, are translated into practice only when the child is invited to co-talk, co-plan, co-construct and co-assess their learning environment together with the teachers and educators.

Children learn everywhere and all the time. To assume that the right type of learning can take place only in a well-structured classroom environment and according to the adult's best thinking is to limit the power of available spaces, local infrastructure and the child's potential. After all, no space or environment should be wasted but instead filled with thought, meaning and action.

6

WHAT SHOULD PARENTS KNOW ABOUT THEIR CHILD'S LEARNING – A FINNISH PERSPECTIVE

Päivi Valtonen (Lic.Ed.), Pedagogical Specialist, Learning Scoop, Tampere, Finland
Johanna Järvinen-Taubert (M.Ed.), Pedagogical Director, Learning Scoop, Tampere, Finland

Finland is world-famous for its excellent results in international education ratings: Finnish children are at the top of the list of best learning results in international comparisons. At the same time, Finland is known to do things very differently in education than most of the other countries. Finnish children experience a happy and stress-free childhood and enjoy short school days and light amount of homework. How can Finnish education be so successful without the pressure and stress? Is there some secret that parents and teachers from other countries could learn from Finland?

In this chapter we share Finnish experiences and debunk common myths about learning and studying. The article also tackles the question many parents have: *How can I support my child's learning the best possible way?*

●●●

How can Finnish education be so successful without the pressure and stress?

●●●

Myths about learning and studying

Myriad world's education conventions are based on certain accepted truths that are rarely challenged:

- Children learn best in teacher-centered instruction where the teacher transfers information to the students.
- Learning requires swotting up.
- The earlier the students start school-like studying, the more and better they learn.
- The more time is spent daily on studying, the better children learn.
- The more homework children have, the more they learn.
- Theoretical subjects are the most important ones at school.

These accepted truths have been debunked in Finnish schools. Moreover, various scientific studies have proven the above-mentioned statements to be false.

Children learn the best with versatile teaching methods

The traditional teacher-centered teaching model is based on the conception of learning that the teacher possesses all the knowledge, and their task is to transfer that knowledge to the students. The teacher speaks, the students listen. The student's task of learning is a lonely one where they merely receive disconnected information. The student is the subject of action, and their role is passive. (Sahlberg & Leppilampi 1994, 21–25.)

Finnish schools do have traditional teacher-led teaching, too. However, there is also a lot of studying based on students' activity and interaction. The children work on projects in pairs or groups, they research phenomena and make videos, comics and plays of what is being learned. Teaching also makes use of different digital applications and learning games. In Finnish schools, the teachers are assumed to utilize other teaching methods besides plain speaking or lecturing. The national core curriculum steers the work of Finnish schools, and states the following on teaching methods:

> *"Versatile working methods bring the pupils joy of learning and experiences of success and support creative activities characteristics of different age groups. Experimental and functional working methods, the engagement of different senses and use of movement increase the experimental nature of learning and strengthen motivation. Motivation is also strengthened by working methods that support self-regulation and feelings of being part of a group."* (National core curriculum for basic education 2014, 31.)

In the traditional teacher-led teaching, the student can obediently listen to the teacher talk, but it does not automatically mean that they would learn anything. Actually, the concept of learning according to modern, scientific research regards learning as an active process by the learner. Learning requires the learner to participate in constructing their own learning: they wonder, enquire, discuss, apply, and use other methods to learn.

> "*Modern learning conception in Finnish education is based on an idea of an active student, eager to gather information, compare and use different methods of learning and to see learning as a process and skill in which it is possible to develop*" (Helminen & Katajamäki 2015).

Learning presupposes understanding

Learning does not presuppose swotting up; it requires understanding and realizing matters and integrating them as a part of a bigger entity. Disconnected details or lists learned by heart are based on memory, and the only way for them to carry meaning is for them to be within the bigger picture.

Learning with understanding means actively constructing information. It is promoted by the learner who ponders upon the matter, asks questions concerning it, wonders at it and explains it to themselves in their own words. Quite often, applying the matter in practice and linking it to one's own experiences plays a role in producing learning with understanding. The new curriculum in Finland emphasizes the use of inquiry-based and phenomenon-based learning methods, both of which promote the students' understanding of greater entities (National core curriculum for basic education 2014, 31–34).

One of the reasons why Finnish children do not need to swot up is that Finnish schools do not have standardized national tests. The teachers can use the time that would otherwise be spent on preparing the children for the tests to focus on teaching broader, more meaningful entities and on truly understand what has been learned.

Playing is more meaningful than starting school early

Finnish children start school significantly later than the children of most other countries. In Finland, the school starting age is seven. At the age of six, children participate in mandatory pre-primary education, before which they have the opportunity to participate in early childhood education and care (ECEC). In Finland, both of these education levels are based on play, activity and developing the children's learning skills. Neither pre-primary education nor early childhood education and care contains school-like studying, subjects or precise class or activity schedules. In pre-primary education, the focus lies on developing the children's learning skills so that starting school would be as easy as possible for them. The targets include promoting children's language skills, stimulate their interest in reading and writing, and developing their learning-to-learn skills. (National Core Curriculum for Pre-primary Education 2016.)

Research has shown that high-quality early childhood education carries a positive effect on children's growth and development, whereas there is no evidence that starting school early would be beneficial (Starting Strong V 2017, 47). On the contrary, various studies have pointed out that free play has a significant impact on children's development (i.a. Whitebread 2012). Activities that are based on playing produce better results than formal, academic teaching (Starting Strong V 2017, 47).

The quality of teaching and learning outweighs the school day's length

Finnish children spend much less time at school than children in other countries. The average school day of a first-grader (in Finland, they would be a 7-year-old) lasts four hours, and weekly hours are approximately 20. The Basic Education Act determines the minimum lesson hours of each grade level. On 1st and 2nd grade, the minimum is 19 hours per week, whereas in lower secondary school (ages 13–15) the weekly minimum is 30 hours.

Among others, Sahlberg (2017, 17) has stated that the hours spent on learning at school do not affect learning results: no positive connection has been established between long-lasting school days and learning results. How much time is spent at school is unimportant; how and what for time is spent is more significant. The quality of teaching and learning and the students' active participation are more important than the hours a student spends at their school.

Loads of homework does not equal more learning

On the international level, Finnish children have fairly light homework. The word *homework* is not mentioned in the Finnish National core curriculum for basic education at all. In the 1–6 grades of primary school (where students' age varies between 7 and 13), children spend a maximum of 30 minutes on doing homework in a day, often even less. Sometimes they have no homework. Additionally, many teachers do not give homework on Fridays since it is the beginning of weekend. There is no homework on holidays, either.

There has been a lot of research on the amount and effectiveness of homework around the world, and the results vary. Cooper (2007), for instance, states that homework tends to benefit older students, not the younger ones who are younger than 10. Cooper's results show that homework develops children's learning and problem-solving skills and self-control. However, the results also suggest that excessive homework load may cause physical and psychological weariness as well as negative attitude towards learning. Having a lot of homework also sets limits to the children's free time. (Cooper 2007; Saloviita 2013, 59.)

PISA surveys have proven Finnish children's excellent performance at school, regardless of their light amount of homework. Saloviita (2013, 59–60) states that each teacher should consider if it is pedagogically justified to give any homework. Homework should, in fact, only be given if there is a pedagogical reason behind it. Homework should always have some kind of a target, like supporting learning or promoting understanding.

Instead of volume, homework should stress quality. Doing a few well-thought exercises that promote learning with understanding or support learning is far more important than completing a great mass of meaningless homework based on mechanical repetition.

All school subjects are important in terms of the children's future

Academic subjects like mother tongue and literature, mathematics, natural sciences, history, and so on are naturally important, but so are the artistic and practical subjects, such as PE, music and visual arts. Approximately one third of all the lessons is dedicated to artistic and practical subjects in Finnish basic education. Artistic and practical subjects also include crafts and home economics in Finland. All students, both girls and boys, participate in crafts and home economics classes equally.

The new Finnish curriculum is founded on the challenges of the future:

> *"We are often asked why improve the system that has been ranked as top quality in the world. But the answer is: because the world is changing. We have to think and rethink everything connected to school. We also have to understand that competencies needed in society and in working life have changed."* (Halinen 2014.)

In order to meet the challenges of the future, the focus in Finland is on generic competencies and especially on work across school subjects. Being good at one specific subject is not enough in the changing world. Students must be able to apply their skills and knowledge to a multitude of contexts. (Halinen 2014.) A child who develops their skills in a versatile manner has an advantage in the future: knowing how to solve unexpected challenges together with others will be even more important in the future.

How can I support my child's learning the best possible way?

Parents cannot influence the standing school system nor the methods of the schools and their teachers, but they can support their child's learning in many different ways. The support of the home and guardians carries a lot of weight in terms of the child's growth, development, and learning. Acknowledging that the parents do not need to be all-knowing superheroes is important; one can encourage their child through very simple and mundane ways, too.

Being accepted and feeling secure form the basis of learning

Regarding children's learning, the parents' interest towards their child's education path and learning is essential. Normally this is the case. The parents want what is best for their child, and it is natural for them to have wishes and expectations for their child's future and success. However, those expectations should not be excessive or put the child under great performance stress. In short, the parents should be interested in the learning of their child, but they should not set excessively high standards for the child's learning and education.

Children learn best when they feel accepted and secure. Each child is unique and should be accepted and loved as they are, even if they would not fulfil all the wishes or expectations of their parents. Moreover, the parents should understand and accept that each child learns at their own pace. Comparing the child with other children or their siblings is not appropriate;

• • •

Children learn best when they feel accepted and secure.

• • •

their development should be compared only with their earlier skills. Comparison with siblings, relatives or schoolmates can easily cause jealousy and negative feelings, as well undermine the child's self-esteem.

Coercion, threats, insults, belittling and physical or psychological violence are even worse starting points for a child's growth, development and learning than comparing them with others. Research shows that this kind of action does not promote learning; it hinders it. Research has pointed out that corporal punishment by parents has a negative impact on children's cognitive development. The negative impact of corporal punishment on children's cognitive development and education may last into adulthood. (Corporal punishment of children: review of research on its impact and associations 2016, 26–27.)

A positive self-image aids learning

Children with a positive self-image of themselves as learners also learn better. The way children form this view – whether they are good or bad learners – is based on the feedback they get from their parents and other meaningful people in their lives. If the child is told that they are lazy or dumb, they will start believing it and act accordingly (the so-called self-fulfilling prophecy).

When giving feedback to a child, it should not be unfounded, superficial praise. Katz (1995) states the following:

> *"Children are unlikely to have their self-esteem strengthened from excessive praise or flattery. On the contrary, it may raise some doubts in children; many children can see through flattery and may even dismiss an adult who heaps on praise, particularly for menial performance, as a poor source of support – one who is not very believable and doesn't believe in their ability to master the difficult."* (Katz 1995.)

There is no need for feedback being only verbal. More often than not, just the genuine presence of the adult who listens to the child and shows their appreciation is enough. If the child has a positive self-image of themselves as a learner, they dare to try.

Above all, the child should be praised for trying, practicing and doing their best, no matter the achieved result. According to research, children who were encouraged to try and praised for their perseverance and hard work, not so much for their good results, were more determined and more aware of the meaning of the hard work. This type of attitude brings along better results in the long run, too.

Research shows that a child who believes that talent is an inborn ability is more likely to give up when facing exercises than a child who believes that traits and skills can be developed. To promote the latter type of attitude, it is helpful to praise the child for trial and error, not so much for their knowledge or success. In fact, a child who is rewarded for trying – regardless of the outcome – has the courage to practice, not only succeed. They learn to believe that they can influence how things turn out and are brave enough to take on a challenge. (Dweck 2006; Heikkinen & Huttu 2017.)

Here are a few examples of meaningful praise:

"That exercise was quite long and complex. It is great that you put your mind into it and dedicated yourself to it!"

"Wow, you are doing so well in natural sciences! You must have practiced a lot."

What is actually "inherited" quite often are the adults' attitudes towards learning. Therefore, it is advisable to speak positively about school and learning, even if there were some negatives experiences, too.

Helping and supporting

Some children require more support than others. The child must be helped when they ask for it. However, they should not be given the correct answers to homework, or have it done by somebody else, as the parent's task is to encourage, guide and help the child in finding the correct answers.

Another important factor is encouraging the child to be persevering and to try. In addition to other research, Sinkkonen (2011) states that giving the child praise on their successful accomplishments does not motivate them to try: if they have already succeeded, there seems to be no point in trying anymore. Instead, expressing admiration for and approval of resolve and good attempt motivates the child to try even harder. (Parvela & Sinkkonen 2011, 111). The appreciation of trying can be seen in the assessment criteria in Finnish basic education: one of them is "I try my best".

Helping a demotivated child

If a child expresses little willingness to learn, the following methods can be used for trying to motivate them:

- Try to awaken the child's interest in the matter at hand. Associate the matter with themes of the child's liking (e.g. linking soccer statistics to mathematics; studying a foreign language in listening to the child's favorite kind of music etc.). Think how you could nourish the child's joy of learning.

- Instruct your child to understand what is being learned rather than trying to remember its details. Those who have understood will remember it better than those who have simply tried to memorize a bunch of detailed facts without understanding their meaning. Discussing the matter together with your child promotes understanding it, as well as trying to put it in a real-life context.
- Praise and encourage your child, especially for trying and persevering. Tell them that you believe they will learn it. Pay special attention to praising them for their effort in learning something.
- Rewards work better than punishment in motivating to learn. Is there something fun for the child to do after they have learned the matter?

In order to help, the parent should also reflect on the reasons behind the child's lack of motivation. Is the school burdening the child too much; are the objectives unrealistic or unclear; does the child get enough of positive learning experiences; how does the child view themselves as a learner; does the child consider learning boring or repetitive struggle and so on.

Co-operation between home and school benefits the child

The teacher should be seen as a co-partner: they share the same objective with the family, which is to help children learn as best as they can. By helping the teacher in succeeding in their work, the children are also given the opportunity to learn as well as possible.

The co-operation between home and school should be a normal part of schoolwork. It should not be problem-oriented, meaning that the teacher only contacts the parents when there is a problem with the child's learning or education. Regular co-operation based on positive interaction guarantees that solving any possible problems is also easy, and it can be done in a constructive manner.

The co-operation of home and school is very versatile in Finnish schools. It is realized as the parents' evening of the whole school or a class, the end-of-term celebration in spring or the Christmas celebration in winter, or various kinds of common events for both parents and children, like the national school-specific "Day of Home and School" in autumn where each school organizes its own activities. In addition to these, daily interaction such as emails, phone calls, pupils' notebooks and communication via electronic systems are a part of the co-operation.

Rest, sleep and recreation also promote learning

We cannot learn when we are tired and weary – this applies to children, too. If the child has long days at school and a lot of homework, it is especially important to ensure that they get enough rest and recreation, too. Research demonstrates that sleep and rest are essential for cognitive functioning, and therefore aid in remembering new information and storing and recalling it (Sallinen 2013; Huotilainen 2019, 184–187). In other words, never compromise your child's rest or sleep!

Children's well-being is constantly a subject for discussion in Finland. Factors such as warm relationships with family and friends, meaningful activities and sufficient physical activity and rest are considered important constituents of well-being. The child should have time for activities they enjoy, whether it be playing with friends or legos, reading or playing an instrument.

Finnish children participate in a lot of hobbies outside of school, but they also have plenty of unorganized free time. Children's free form playing is highly esteemed in Finland, and it is seen as an important source of learning. Having time to simply be without any special plans or performance stress is essential to children.

Learning is fun!

The joy of learning is a widely discussed topic in Finland. It is mentioned as one of the objectives of education in the national core curriculum (National core curriculum for basic education 2014, 31). Each child, regardless of their abilities or competencies, should have the right to experience the joy of learning. Everybody can always learn something new! The joy of learning is derived from discovering something new, mastering new skills, working and trying, collaborating, reaching personal targets as well as the unforced, motivation-oriented curiosity and exploring.

The best way to promote the learning of your child is to rejoice together in the new things that they have learned. You can support your child's learning by encouraging their wondering, curious attitude and sharing the moments and feelings of learning something new with them. Children learn a great deal from the adults around them. If the adults show an eager and positive attitude towards learning new and exploring the wonders of the world, the children will then adapt similar attitudes. So, take part in the joy of learning with your child!

References

Cooper, H. 2007. *The battle over homework: Common ground for administrators, teachers, and parents.* Thousand Oaks: Corwin Press.

Corporal punishment of children: review of research on its impact and associations 2016. Global Initiative to End All Corporal Punishment of Children. Working paper June 2016.

Dweck, C. S. 2006. *Mindset: The New Psychology of Success. How can we learn to fulfill our potential.* New York: Random House.

Halinen, I. 2014. General aspects of basic education curriculum reform

2016 Finland. Finnish National Board of Education. Accessed 12 March 2020. Retrieved from https://www.youtube.com/watch?v=KY_LZJkEo28

Heikkinen, K., & Huttu, T. 2017. *Pää edellä – Näin tuet lapsesi aivojen kehitystä* [The head first – How to support the child's brain development]. Helsinki: WSOY.

Helminen, L., & Katajamäki, M. 2015. An Introduction to Teaching in Finland for International Staff. FIS-STEPS Project.

Huotilainen, M. 2019. *Näin aivot oppivat* [How the brain learns]. Jyväskylä: PS-kustannus.

Katz, L. 1995. How can we strengthen children's self-esteem. ERIC Clearinghouse on Elementary and Early Childhood Education.

National core curriculum for basic education 2014 2016. Finnish National Board of Education. Publications 5. Helsinki.

National Core Curriculum for Pre-primary Education 2014 2016. Finnish National Board of Education. Publications 6. Helsinki.

Parvela, T., & Sinkkonen, J. 2011. Kouluun! Ekaluokkalaisen vanhemmille [To the school! For a first-grader's parents]. Helsinki: WSOY.

Sahlberg, P., & Leppilampi, A. 1994. Yksinään vai yhteisvoimin? Yhdessäoppimisen mahdollisuuksia etsimässä [Alone or together? In search of opportunities for learning together]. Vantaa: Helsingin yliopisto [Helsinki University].

Sahlberg, P. 2017. Finnished leadership. Four big, inexpensive ideas to transform education. Corwin.

Sallinen, M. 2013. Uni, muisti ja oppiminen [Sleep, memory and learning]. Lääketieteellinen Aikakauskirja [Medical science periodical] Duodecim 129 (21), 2253–2259.

Saloviita, T. (Ed.) 2013. Luokka haltuun! Parhaat keinot toimivaan opetukseen [Manage your class! The best tools for effective teaching]. Jyväskylä: PS-kustannus.

Starting Strong V 2017. Transitions from Early Childhood Education and Care to Primary Education. OECD Publishing.

Whitebread, D. 2012. The importance of play. A report on the value of children's play with a series of policy recommendations. University of Cambridge.

7

EPILOGUE: THE FUTURE OF EDUCATION

Riitta Juusenaho (PhD, Ed.), Trainer, TOP School Consulting, Kangasala, Finland

"The winds are favorable for those who know where they are going." Vasco da Gama (1460–1524)

One great teacher can be the sole savior of an otherwise unhappy childhood, but a whole group of great teachers can work together and save the child's whole life and help them in their first steps! Even though this might sound like a cliché, the truth behind it cannot be dismissed. When teachers work together, their common competence grows exponentially. Co-operation brings along continuity and new perspectives which teachers might not notice alone. On top of that, co-operation shelters individual teachers from burn-outs.

The present book on Finnish education and its practices is a great example of pedagogical co-operation. All its authors work close to everyday school life either as teachers, principals, vice-principals, adult educators or researchers, and each of them has extensive professional competence in training international operators with an interest in Finnish education within the field, both home and abroad. Every author has encountered the same question during their work in these arenas: What is it that is being done in the schools of the small Nordic country of Finland that year by year brings the country's high quality and effectiveness forth as one of the best ones in the world? In these articles, the authors share their views and experiences of their work as Finnish teachers and experts within the field of education.

When it comes to the quality and authority of education, the most central role is that of the teacher. However, other important aspects to consider include the educational-policy structures, systems, and spaces within and by whom education is realized. The national core curricula, a collaborative effort of hundreds of Finnish teachers, create an equal base that guides how the municipalities and cities build their own operations models while simultaneously taking legislation into account. Higher education, broad pedagogical competence, and the community's deep, complete trust in them ensure Finnish teachers' autonomic freedom to realize instruction in their classrooms or outside of them, without the burden of supervisors standing over them or having to fill masses of reports.

The principals' duty is not limited to enabling all the above-mentioned factors only, but also to lead the way as innovators and the source of continuous pedagogical advancement. Finnish principals are running their schools in the forefront, not behind them. For this very reason, they are required, in addition to teacher's education, education in leadership, administration and legislation as well as people management (Juusenaho 2004; Lahtero, Ahtiainen & Lång 2019). A successful principal is also skilled in pedagogical leadership; they understand the meaning of following the national curriculum's realization, not forgetting the meaning of developing the school culture as a whole for the sake of all the persons working within it.

This book sheds light on the Finnish education system by candidly depicting the work of the multidisciplinary professionals within the field with illustrating examples from real life. These authentic examples are, in my opinion, the greatest offer of this book. As the book's title states, its intention is to answer the questions of *what*, *why* and *how*.

The future of education

The world is fast-forwarding ever more rapidly, which makes pausing and considering what the future for which we are preparing ourselves is like with regard to education even more important. The challenges – and possibilities

• • •

When it comes to the quality and authority of education, the most central role is that of the teacher.

• • •

– of globalization, the turning point in working life, digitalization and the undeniable inequality growing both inside and between societies invites education, too, to look at its own working principles with a critical eye. The essential questions of "what is learned" and "how is learned" are crucial to planning. It has been said that education is always to plan the future (Sitra 2017).

The greatest societal challenges are complicated by nature. Predicting the future is not easy, but societal planning is both reasonable and necessary. According to the report by Sitra, the Finnish Innovation Fund, the school system should strive for deep learning that changes how the world is viewed and raise people with such skills, abilities and attitudes that enable them to take up complex challenges and find solutions to them (Cook 2018). This can be achieved only if we accept the fact that there is an existing need for the continuous improving of the national curricula.

Many countries have been talking about the so-called 21st Century Skills in education for a while now. The term refers to the idea that instead of the behaviorist culture of memorization and repetition, instruction and education should focus on teaching and learning skills.

In fact, the main idea of the Finnish National core curriculum for basic education (2016) is comprehensive learning, which is closely associated with learning the above-mentioned skills. The way of thinking and working, the mastery of various tools and participatory citizenship have been established as the framework of these skills.

The way of thinking means, above all, the ability to solve problems and innovate creatively, and to dare to trial and learn from the errors.

The way of working means, above all, the ability to collaborate, learn from one another and communicate.

Mastery of tools in the Finnish curriculum means critical reading, media literacy, educational technology and both information and communication skills among others.

Participatory citizenship means active participation in society, internationality, life management abilities, social responsibility, and a sustainable lifestyle.

These skills can hardly be successfully learned only by reading books or listening to the teacher talk. Learning processes must therefore be created as much as possible in reality-like situations, in which, in the mind of a young child, the skills that are being learned are associated with real-life situations. In addition to learning environments, this imposes demands to the teachers, too, who must be competent in various pedagogical ways of teaching while also being skilled in observing the alertness level of their students. This also necessitates a change in the roles of both the teacher and the student.

Now, the teacher is no longer the sole owner of knowledge, and the fact must be accepted that learning occurs outside of the borders of the classroom and school, too. The socio-constructivist approach currently prevailing in Finland emphasizes that learning is a social, interactive and collaborative process which puts the learner in the center of the learning process as an active participant (subject) who then builds their own reality by constructing new information based and on top of previous knowledge. Information is thus always constructed by either the individual or the community. The teacher must accept the different realities of the students because their social contexts (homes, friends, family members, hobbies etc.) shape their frames for constructing new information in different ways.

"In this era of abundant information and contradictions, the people who will run the world are those who can synthesize information by picking up the essential puzzle pieces and arranging them into a meaningful pattern." SITRA 2018

The future poses a challenge to the co-operation between education and working life. We are in the middle of educating young people into a world that we know little about; we are training them for professions that do not even exist yet. That is why it is important that older students are familiarized with the contents of working life as early as in the upper grades of basic education and on a deeper level than they are today. If this is done, they will be aware of the important educational possibilities when it comes to their further education. The prerequisite for this is even closer future co-operation between schools and local businesses. In consequence, we can better avoid wrong choices in the education path, save resources and shorten the period of study. From now on teachers, too, should be even more aware of the needs and routines of working life at all levels of education, including academic universities. School must never remain an isolated island with its own life but must become a more and more integral part of society.

Rapid and accelerating changes in the operational environments, such as regional inequality, changes in family dynamics, changes in work and its insecurity, or the climate change will challenge planning in the future, upon which political decisions are based. Technologization of working life requires continuous learning of the workforce, and employers need to prepare themselves to continuously train their employees. It is anticipated that in the future, a person might have to train for up to three to four different occupations before retiring. It is therefore essential that education providers are also able to anticipate and adapt to the various future needs of each society's working life, societal challenges, environmental issues and sustainable development by guaranteeing the pupils and students educators who are as competent teachers as possible.

In a seminar organized by Sitra (2017), Finnish professor Markku Wilenius listed seven principles for future schools and companies for developing their activities in a more proactive and future-oriented direction:

1. Hierarchies should be forgotten, and sharing knowledge should be enabled.
2. Instead of technical skills, emphasis should be placed on social and systemic skills.
3. Organizations' separate innovation departments are closed. Innovating and learning new things becomes the new normal.
4. Radical solutions are embraced.
5. A commitment is made to consider matters far into the future.
6. Risks are taken.
7. The future is viewed as a mission.

"Education is not the learning of facts, but the training of the mind to think."
Albert Einstein (1879–1955)

School hierarchies will be further diminished in the future. Principals will increasingly be required to have vision and a desire for shared leadership. As a consequence, employers must also take into account the increasing need for in-service training for principals. Principals' work will be more dynamic and more rapidly changing leadership that demands the ability of tolerating incompleteness (Juusenaho, 2004, 59; Ouakrim-Soivio et al. 2015, 87–89).

School staff will even more extensively include support service providers, too, such as psychologists, school social workers, assistants, social workers, doctors, counselors, and hobby coaches. A successful future education system understands the importance of knowledge transfer and collegial collaboration. Barriers of knowledge transfer have been cleared, and the objective is to detect learners' problems at an ever earlier stage and to take personal support measures in daily school life.

Social skills and the ability to work together with one another will be a prerequisite for future work. Fewer and fewer of us will be working alone in the future. The role of teamwork and self-directedness will be further emphasized, and those who possess these skills will be even more attractive employees in the labor market. It is therefore vital to start practicing these skills as early as in early childhood education.

The humane fear of failure often prevents us from trying out a new way of teaching or learning. In the future, however, it is through these failures that something completely new can be created, which is why various experimentations need to be an intrinsic part of school life. Sometimes rules need to be broken in order to make progress. Taking conscious – not reckless – risks should be allowed. If there is one thing, we can be sure of, it is that nothing really changes if we only take the paths that have already been travelled. In addition to this, teachers also need to learn even more from each other and share their good practices.

Education contributes to the well-being and competitiveness of the whole society. Confidence in the future, broad-mindedness, self-development, co-operation, and the feeling of being accepted are the building blocks of progress. Nevertheless, these building blocks must be backed up by a continuous opportunity to learn new throughout life. Being curious and believing in oneself are the driving forces of humanity.

When envisioning the future of education and its needs for change, the necessity to develop education evaluation must also be taken into account. As the operating culture of school changes, evaluation practices must be changed as well.

In the future, the evaluation of learning should focus increasingly on qualitative efficiency evaluation, in addition to quantitative monitoring. Both local and school-specific evaluation practices, a general evaluation culture that includes generally accepted evaluation methods, and conventions concerning their use in quality development must be established. Similarly, the evaluation skills of all those involved in work within the education field must be developed.

The assessment of young pupils will focus more deeply on qualitative measures. The pupil's overall development and growth as a human being is at the heart of assessment. For older students, their competence assessment will be emphasized by evidence-based methods.

The socio-constructivist learning approach underlines students' personal way of constructing and creating information. In a similar manner, the nature of evaluation will change so that it focuses more on individual characteristics and both assess and support the individual's learning process.

In terms of the quality and effectiveness of future education, the communities and societies that develop their education systems as a coherent whole, not just various pieces, will have a head start.

References

Cook J.W. (Ed.) 2018. *Sustainability, Human Well-being and the Future of Education. London:* Palgrave Macmillan.

Juusenaho, R, 2004. Differences in comprehensive school leadership and management. A gender-based approach. University of Jyväskylä, Department of Education. Jyväskylä Studies in Education, Psychology and Social Research 249. In Finnish.

Lahtero, T., Ahtiainen, S., & Lång, N. 2019. Finnish principals: Leadership training and views on distributed leadership. *Educational Research and Reviews, 14* (10), 340–348.

National core curriculum for basic education 2014 2016. Finnish National Board of Education. Publications 5. Helsinki.

Ouakrim-Soivio, N., Rinkinen, A., & Karjalainen, T. (Ed.) 2015. Tulevaisuuden peruskoulu [The school of the future]. Opetus- ja kulttuuriministeriön julkaisuja [Publications by the Ministy of Education and Culture] 2015:8.

Sitra 2017. Koulutus on tulevaisuuden ennakointia [Education is the prediction of the future]. Accessed on 03 March 2020. Retrieved from https://www.sitra.fi/blogit/koulutus-tulevaisuuden-ennakointia/

Sitra 2018. Kansainvälinen tutkijaryhmä: Kestävä tulevaisuus koulutuksen tärkeimmäksi tehtäväksi [International research group: Sustainable future as the most important task of education]. Accessed on 03 March 2020. Retrieved from https://www.sitra.fi/uutiset/kansainvalinen-tutkijaryhma-kestava-tulevaisuus-koulutuksen-tarkeimmaksi-tehtavaksi/

EDUCATION SYSTEM IN FINLAND

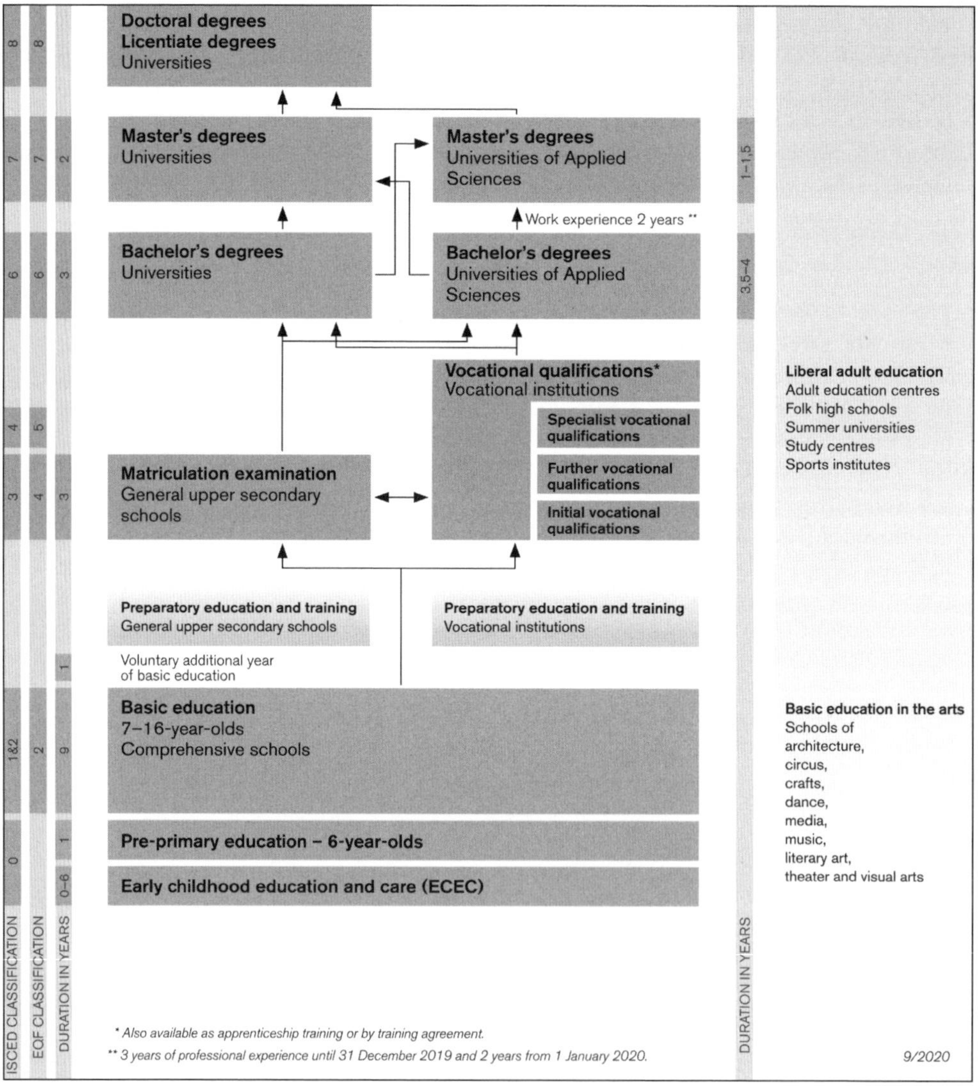

Source: https://minedu.fi/en/education-system

FACTS ABOUT FINNISH EDUCATION

- Every child in Finland has a subjective right to attend early childhood education and care if the family so wishes. It can take place at kindergartens or smaller family day-care groups in private homes. Pre-primary education is compulsory for children at the age of six.
- Basic education in Finland lasts altogether nine years, between 7 and 16 years. Basic education is provided within a single structure: there is no division into primary and lower secondary education.
- Instruction in basic education is usually given by the same class teacher in most subjects in the first six year-classes and by different subject specialists in the last three years in basic education.
- In Finland, the teaching and guidance staff within early childhood education and care generally have Bachelor's degrees. Pre-primary teachers and teachers in basic and general upper secondary education are required to hold a Master's degree.
- The national core curricula for early childhood education, pre-primary education, basic education and general upper secondary education are determined by the Finnish National Agency for Education.
- All basic education schools in Finland follow the respective national core curriculum. There are no national tests for pupils in basic education in Finland.
- After basic education, students continue to secondary education, usually to general upper secondary school or vocational upper secondary education and training. General upper secondary education ends with a

national matriculation examination, which is the first and only national examination of the Finnish education system.

- Education in Finland is free of charge at all levels, all the way from pre-primary education to higher education.
- Most institutions providing basic and upper secondary level education are maintained by local authorities or joint municipal consortia.
- All schools in Finland are publicly funded; there are no tuition fees.
- There are no gender-based schools in Finland: all schools have both boys and girls as students.
- In Finland, special needs education is primarily provided in mainstream education, not in separate special education schools.
- The Finnish education system has no dead-ends. Learners can always continue their studies on an upper level education, no matter what choices they make in between.
- Higher education is offered by universities and universities of applied sciences. Universities emphasize scientific research and instruction, whereas universities of applied sciences have adopted a more practical approach.
- Adult education is very popular in Finland – the participation rate is high also in international terms.

References

Finnish Education in a Nutshell 2017. Finland's Ministry of Education and Culture and Finnish National Agency for Education. Accessed on 15 April 2021. Retrieved from https://www.oph.fi/sites/default/files/documents

INDEX

L

M

N

O

P

JOHANNA JÄRVINEN-TAUBERT

Master of Education, Teacher qualification

Promoting learning in different ways and contexts has been at the core of Johanna Järvinen-Taubert's work. She has worked as a teacher trainer and university researcher in the field of education. For the last 20 years, she has trained teachers from early childhood education, basic education, high schools, and higher education in Finnish in-service teacher training programs. This has given her comprehensive insight into the Finnish education system. Among others, Johanna's fields of expertise also include developing teaching and learning methods.

Over the past years as a pedagogical director, Johanna has focused on training foreign teachers, students and education experts on Finnish education. Her mission is to share ideas and best practices with experts from other countries.

PÄIVI VALTONEN

Licentiate of Education

Since her graduation, Päivi Valtonen has accumulated over twenty years of experience in the field of education. Moreover, she has worked as a researcher at the University of Tampere in Finland. The main focus of her research has been the effectiveness of education.

Päivi has extensive practical knowledge of both early childhood education and basic education. She has also trained university students as well as teachers of all school levels in Finnish in-service teacher training programs. Her core competence lies in pedagogy: the planning of further education for teachers in addition to designing learning materials and contents for pedagogical courses. Päivi truly believes that teaching is a helping profession: when teaching, the main concern is assisting learners to learn and develop themselves.

ELENA CHUKHLANTSEVA

Master of Education, Teacher qualification

Elena Chukhlantseva has gained over twenty years of academic and practical experience in multicultural and multilingual educational settings. She is a trained English language teacher and class teacher. What's more, she holds a master's degree in International and Comparative Education, specializing in Educational Leadership and Management. In addition to having conducted scientific research in the field of sociology of education, she has taught in both Finnish and bilingual early childhood education centers and schools while also co-managing an early childhood education center.

Elena has trained teachers, experts and other relevant stakeholders both in Finland and abroad. As an ECEC Specialist, Elena has emphasized training others on Finnish early year and primary education; collaborating with partners in developing a Finland-inspired curriculum for early year education; and promoting the best Finnish educational practices.